ISBN 978-1-330-58514-6
PIBN 10032415

English
Français
Deutsche
Italiano
Español
Português

www.forgottenbooks.com

Mythology Photography **Fiction**
Fishing Christianity **Art** Cooking
Essays Buddhism Freemasonry
Medicine **Biology** Music **Ancient
Egypt** Evolution Carpentry Physics
Dance Geology **Mathematics** Fitness
Shakespeare **Folklore** Yoga Marketing
Confidence Immortality Biographies
Poetry **Psychology** Witchcraft
Electronics Chemistry History **Law**
Accounting **Philosophy** Anthropology
Alchemy Drama Quantum Mechanics
Atheism Sexual Health **Ancient History**
Entrepreneurship Languages Sport
Paleontology Needlework Islam
Metaphysics Investment Archaeology
Parenting Statistics Criminology
Motivational

THE
Story of an Ancient Parish

BREAGE WITH GERMOE,

With some account of its
Armigers, Worthies and
Unworthies, Smugglers
and Wreckers, Its
Traditions and Superstitions

BY

H. R. COULTHARD, M.A.

1913.

THE CAMBORNE PRINTING AND STATIONERY COMPANY, LIMITED,
CAMBORNE, CORNWALL.

I dedicate this small volume to the friends and neighbours who in the first place suggested the writing of it to me by telling me stories of the days of their fathers.

CONTENTS.

LIST OF ILLUSTRATIONS.

PREFACE.

THE facts and thoughts which comprise this little book were many of them, in the first instance, arranged for use in sermons on the Sundays preceding our local Feast Day, as some attempt to interest Parishioners in the story of our Church and parish.

I have to acknowledge with gratitude much information given me most ungrudgingly, from his great store of anti-quarian learning, by the Reverend T. Taylor, Vicar of St. Just; likewise my thanks are due to Mr. H. Jenner for kindly help and information upon the etymology of local place names. I must also acknowledge the free use I have made of facts bearing upon the history of Breage and Germoe taken from Mr. Baring-Gould's " Historic Characters and Events in Cornwall," and at the same time I have to express my thanks to the Reverend H. J. Warner, Vicar of Yealmpton, the Reverend H. G. Burden, Vicar of Leominster, and Mr. A. E. Spender for valuable information and assistance. I have been greatly helped in my examination of the Parish Registers by the excellent transcription of large parts of them made by Mrs. Jocelyn Barnes. Finally I have to thank a great number of kind friends at Breage, who have imparted to me the fast fading traditions of other times, to whom I venture to dedicate this brief record of days that are no more.

Breage,
All Saints' Day, 1912.

LIST OF THE VICARS OF BREAGE.

Date of Institution.		
—	WILLIAM, Son of Richard ...	Died or resigned during the Interdict
1219	WILLIAM, Son of Humphrey ...	
1264	Master ROBERT DE LA MORE ...	Resigned to become Canon of Glasney, ultimately parson of Yeovil.
1264	Master STEPHENUS DE ARBOR	
—	Sir PASCASIUS	No date of Institution. Old, blind and infirm in 1310.
1313	Sir DAVID DE LYSPEIN ...	
—	Sir JOHN YURL DE TREGESOU	No date of Institution.
1362	HENRY CRETTIER	
—	Sir WILLIAM PELLOUR ...	No date of Institution.
1393	Sir JOHN GODE	Died at Breage.
1403	Master WILLIAM PENSANS ...	Died at Breage.
1439	Sir JOHN PATRY	Died at Breage.
1444	Sir JOHN PEYTO	Died at Breage.
1445	Sir WILLIAM LEHE	Died at Breage.
1466	Sir WILLIAM PERS	Resigned to become Canon of Glasney
1505	Master THOMAS GODOLPHIN ...	Resigned.
1510	Master JOHN JAKES, Bachelor in Decrees	Died at Breage.
1536	JOHN BERY, M.A.	Died at Breage.
1558	Sir ALEXANDER DAWE ...	Died at Breage.
1595	FRANCIS HARVEY, M.A. ...	Vicar also of St. Erth, buried in Breage Churchyard.
1607	WILLIAM COTTON, M.A. ...	Son of the Bishop of Exeter, resigned, holder of many other benefices in Devon and Cornwall.
1608	WILLIAM ORCHARD, "Preacher of the Word of God."	Resigned.
	JAMES INNES (ejected 1661) ...	Intruding Puritan Divine.
1661	JAMES TREWINNARD, M.A. ...	Resigned on becoming Vicar of Mawgan, at which place he lies buried
1696	HENRY HUTHNANCE	Died at Breage, lies buried beyond the East wall of the chancel.
1720	JAMES TREWINNARD, M.A. ...	Died at Breage, also Vicar of Mawgan.
1722	EDWARD COLLINS, Bachelor of Laws	Died at Breage, also Vicar of St. Erth, where he lies buried.
1755	HENRY USTICKE, B.A.	Died at Breage, lies buried beyond the East wall of the chancel.
1769	EDWARD MARSHALL, M.A. ...	Died at Breage.
1803	RICHARD GERVEYS GRYLLS, M.A	Resigned.
1809	RICHARD GERVEYS GRYLLS, M.A., the younger	Died at Luxulian, which parish he held in conjunction with Breage.
1853	EDWARD MORRIS PRIDMORE. M.A.	Died at Breage.
1889	JOCELYN BARNES, M.A. ...	Died at Breage.
1904	HARRY JOHN PETTY	Resigned.
1907	HUGH ROBERT COULTHARD. M.A.	

THE CELTIC PERIOD.

CHAPTER I.

A T the dawn of history, Cornwall, as in fact England generally, was inhabited by a race of small, dark people, who, for the want of a better name, have come to be called Ivernians. The blood of this ancient dark race chiefly survives to-day in South Wales and Cornwall, especially in our own western Cornwall along the coast line. In Breage, there are continually to be met with faces and forms which suggest this small dark race, and which show to what a large extent the ancient Ivernian blood still survives in our midst.

The Ivernians must have been widely spread over Cornwall, judging by the numerous chippings from the manufacture of their flint implements scattered all over the County, which still may be collected in large quantities. In spite of the continuous mining operations carried on all over the Parish of Breage for endless generations, and the many ploughings of the land which must have taken place in periods when the growth of grain was profitable, these flint chippings can still be gathered in many places in the parish, especially on the bare patches of land where the gorse has been burnt, before the grass begins to spring. In the earlier stages of their history the Ivernians used sharpened fragments of flint rudely fashioned to the purpose, as knives, axes and scrapers. In fact, for a long period of their history they were a people living in and under the conditions of the Stone Age.

Long before the time of written records another race,

called Celts, found their way to Cornwall. This race was divided into two distinct branches, the Goidels and the Brythons. The Goidels were much inferior in culture to the Brythons; they were the first to enter Britain, and upon the arrival of the Brythons they were slaughtered and driven before them to the remote fastnesses of the West and North, just as in a later age the Brythons themselves were driven before the Saxons. Under the circumstances it might have been reasonable to conclude that the people of Cornwall, in so far as they were not Ivernians, were mainly of Goidelic blood. This conclusion is, however, not borne out by the Cornish language which has come down to us in the form of a few miracle plays and other fragments, which is undoubtedly Brythonic in character. Of course, it may have been that, when the Brythons were driven into Cornwall and Wales and across the Channel into Brittany in hordes by the remorseless, exterminating Saxons, their tongue in these regions gradually supplanted the more barbarous Goidelic speech.

The Celts, as they advanced westward, whether Goidel or Brython, would exterminate or make slaves of the Ivernians, driving them before them as they advanced into the extreme western parts of the County. We have all heard a number of foolish stories of the Cornish folk in the fishing villages being largely descended from Spanish soldiers and sailors who were saved from wrecked battleships of the great Armada. These fisher folk are dark and swarthy, not because they are descended from Spaniards but because they are descended from the ancient Ivernians who took refuge in the caves and rugged places along the coast, leaving the good land to the conquering Celts.

The Celts, we imagine, would find the Ivernians professing a rude system of natural religion much akin to their own, but perhaps not so highly developed; indeed, a very large proportion of the human race at this far distant time seems to have practised a religion of nature worship alike in its main features. Here in Cornwall, as elsewhere, for instance, they kept a great festival in the spring-time, when they celebrated the coming to life again of the God of vegetation, whose name amongst the Celts was Gwydian.* He was supposed to come to life again with the coming of the green grass, the leaves and the flowers, and the singing of the birds, having died in the previous autumn with the withering of the leaves and the in-gathering of the harvest. Helston Flora Day is the festival of his resurrection continued right down through the ages. As in spring they rejoiced over the resurrection of the God of vegetation, so in autumn they mourned over his death.† Most of us have heard the old Cornish rhyme sung by the reapers at the cutting of the last sheaf, which is a survival of this ancient custom of bewailing the death of Gwydian.

> " I'll have un, I'll have un, I'll have un,
> What have'e, What have'e, What have'e,
> What will'e, What will'e, What will'e,
> Onec, Onec, Onec, O'hurro, O'hurro, O'hurro."

As this rhyme was repeated, all the harvesters stood round the farmer in a circle, whilst he waved a sheaf in the air. This custom of mourning the dead God of vegetation was very widely spread over the world.‡ No one who has heard the mournful strain in which this chant of our ancient harvest fields was sung can doubt that in its original use it was a song of mourning.

The Celtic Priests or Druids knew a good deal of rude astronomy. They used the stone circles, so many of which still survive, for purposes of astronomical observations. By watching the alignment of the sun at rising or setting, and also of certain stars, with the centre stone and some stone on

---

*See Professor Rhys "Origin and growth of Celtic Religion" pp. 225, 236, 245.
†See Frazer's "Attis, Adonis and Osiris."
‡See Frazer's "Attis, Adonis and Osiris."

the circumference of the circle, they were able to calculate the seasons of the year and the dates of their festivals. Until a generation ago one of these ancient circles stood on Trewarvas Head ; it was pulled down by some foolish and ignorant people who thought they might find hidden treasure under the great stones. From the top of the high cliff overlooking the sea the Druid Priests would have a splendid view of the far horizon. We can picture them making their observations through the silent hours of some still star-lit night, with the ceaseless slumbrous swell of the sea on the rocks far beneath them.

On Midsummer Eve the Druids lit a great fire on the summit of Tregoning Hill. We know this, because the custom of lighting the fire survived until very recent times. An old woman deplored its discontinuance to the writer as a sign of the prevailing irreligion of the times. It seems more than probable that at this Midsummer Festival human victims were sometimes sacraficed in honour of the sun.

In the remote Highlands and Islands of Scotland this festival was observed down to the early part of the eighteenth century, in a way which clearly points to human sacrifice as the great central act of the rite.[*] Numbers of men were in the habit of gathering on Midsummer Eve in these remote parts of the kingdom round the ancient stone circles midst the hills. A fire was lighted in the centre of the circle ; pieces of cake or bannock were then placed in some cavity where previously a blackened and burnt fragment of the cake had been placed. Each person, having first been blindfolded, then drew from the cavity a piece of the broken cake ; the man unfortunate enough to draw the blackened fragment had to leap through the fire and pay a forfeit or fine. In the dim past the drawer of the blackened fragment doubtless became

---

[*]Account by Revd. Alexander Hislop, Minister of Arbroath in "The Two Babylons."

the victim offered to the God to ward off his anger from the community. This ancient rite must have been practised in our Parish more than a thousand years before the coming of Christ.

At the very dawn of human history we find all over the world, in Europe, India, China and America, the ancient peoples keeping four great festivals as a rule, at the summer and winter solstices and the two equinoxes ; in fact their religious culture in cardinal points was one and the same.

One part of the faith of these ancient Ivernians and Celts that has lingered on to our own times is the deeply cherished belief in Fairies. How this belief came to be so widely spread and deeply cherished amongst ancient peoples it is impossible to say. It has been suggested that, in their wanderings over the world in search of pasturage and congenial climate, they may have encountered in the recesses of primeval forests or in lonely fastnesses of the mountains remnants of the slowly vanishing pigmy race of neo-lithic cave men, and that they came to regard them with something of superstitous awe, and that the memory of these "little people" became a race memory, in the course of generations becoming etherealised and woven into the woof of their religious beliefs. On the other hand we have the possible view that our nomadic forefathers may have had fitful glimpses, as some of their descendants aver they have, of orders of beings beyond the ken of normal human vision, of beings existing upon another plane. Taking into consideration the exceeding aboundingness of human life within the radius of our poor faculties, I confess that this view seems to present no inherent difficulty.

Possibly in the way in which the people of each Cornish Parish possessed in former generations a nickname, we have a vestige of still more ancient rights, which carry us back to the very dawn of human culture. We have Wendron goats, Mullion gulls, Madron bulls, St. Agnes cuckoos, Mawgan owls, St. Keverne buccas† and many others. The following old rhyme perpetuates the fading memory of the custom,

"Cambourne men are bull dogs,
Breage men are brags,
Germoe men can scat 'un all to rags."

An analogous custom to this Cornish system of nick-names prevails amongst primitive people all the world over.‡ Each tribe or section of the tribe has its Totem, an animal, bird or plant, with which it is supposed to be in close and intimate relationship, and from which the tribe or section of a tribe receives its name. Possibly Totemism may have had its origin in crude attempts of primitive men to prevent too close intermarriage, as men and women possessing the same Totem were not allowed to marry, whilst on the other hand it has been suggested that the custom was bound up with the view of primitive men with regard to sacrifice and inter-communion with their Gods.

The Tin Mines of Cornwall had been known to the Greeks and possibly the Phœnicians from the earliest times. Diodorus *Siculus gives a fragment from the writings of the Greek traveller Poseidonius who visited Cornwall possibly in the 3rd century B.C., which may be translated as follows : "and stamping the tin into shapes of cubes or dice, they carry it in great quantities in waggons into an island called Ictis lying off Britain, when the parts between the Island and the main land became dry land by the ebbing of the tide."

It has been suggested that Ictis was St. Michael's Mount

---

†Bucca connected with Scottish "Bogle." Bogle always in Scotland means a disembodied spirit. Bucca with Bogle said to be akin to Sclavonic "Bog" i.e. God, We incline to think Cornish "bucca" and Scottish "bogle" may be taken as equivalent in meaning. See Wentz "Fairy Faith of Celtic Countries" pp. 164 and 165.

‡See Andrew Lang "Secret of the Totem." Also W. Gregory "The Dead Heart of Australia" pp. 188 to 195.

* "ἀποτυποῦντες δ' εἰς ἀστραγάλων ῥυθμοὺς κομίζουσιν εἰς νῆσον προκειμένην τῆς Βρεττανικῆς, ὀνομαζομένην δὲ Ἴκτιν. κατὰ γὰρ ἀμπώτεις ἀναξηραινομένου τοῦ μεταξὺ τόπου, ταῖς ἁμάξαις εἰς ταύτην κομίζουσι τὸν κασσίτερον δαψιλῆ."

Diodorus Siculus.

and also the Isle of Wight. It is impossible to accept the latter contention, unless we take the view which has been put forward that great changes have taken place in the depths of the channel separating the Isle of Wight from the mainland, for which we have no evidence in history or tradition. Also the Isle of Wight is not less than one hundred and fifty miles from the tin mines of Cornwall, and at the period to which we are referring the only roads that existed between the two were mere tracks, for much of the distance no doubt impassable to waggons. If it had been necessary to send Cornish tin to the Isle of Wight for transport abroad, it would naturally have been taken to one or other of the many harbours along the Cornish southern coast and transhipped by sea in the summer time. The contention in favour of St. Michael's Mount is almost equally difficult to accept. It is difficult to see what advantage could have been gained by carting the tin from the mainland to that Island, when the contiguous coast possessed several excellent natural harbours. The most probable solution to the writer seems to be that the Island of Ictis was the entire Penwith Peninsula. A walk from Marazion Station to St. Erth along the low-lying belt of marsh land makes it clear that the ocean at no very distant date must at high tide have encircled the Penwith Peninsula.

In a later age it is possible that the first seeds of Christianity may have come to Britain by way of Cornwall along the trade route created by the exportation of the products of the Cornish Tin Mines to Marseilles. Foreign merchants would visit Cornwall for the purpose of purchasing tin, and numbers of foreign sailors would come to these shores in the galleys that conveyed the tin to the coast of Gaul. Under the circumstances it does not seem unreasonable to suppose that the first seeds of Christianity were in this way brought into Britain through Cornwall.

It seems in every way possible that a fair proportion of

the tin exported from the Island of Ictis to Greece, Italy and the East came from what is now the Parish of Breage. We have been told by those competent to speak on such matters that there are tin workings in the neighbourhood of Wheal Vor which evince a very great antiquity. The name of Wheal Vor itself means in the Celtic tongue " great work,' but we cannot build much as to the antiquity of the mine merely upon its Celtic name, as the Cornish or Celtic language continued to be spoken in this part of Cornwall even until the reign of Queen Anne or later.

At what date the Romans penetrated into Cornwall it is impossible to say. It has been usual to regard their occupation of Cornwall as of a somewhat shadowy and uncertain character, but this is not altogether borne out by facts. Their camps, possibly of a not very permanent character, are scattered all over our most western part of the County, amongst other places there is one at St. Erth and another in the parish of Constantine. The Roman Mile-stone, found in the foundations of St. Hilary Church, at the restoration, and now preserved there, attests the fact that a Roman road to the extreme West passed near St. Hilary Church, probably following the same lines that the main road between Penzance and Helston follows to-day. Along this road it is probable would come the first real light and culture to Breage with the steady tramp of the marching legionaries. It may well have been that Christianity first travelled this way in their train. Roman coins and Roman pottery have been from time to time found all over the County. In 1779 an urn containing copper coins weighing eight pounds was found on Godolphin Farm by a ploughman who sold them to a Jew, and so all trace of them was lost.

In whatever way Christianity was first brought to the remote Parish of Breage, it was certainly not brought by St. Breaca, St. Germoe and the rest of their companions, who only made their appearance at the end of the fifth or beginning of the sixth century.

As early as the third century two great Christian writers, Tertullian and Origen, speak of the Britons as having been won over to the religion of Christ, and St. Chrysostom in the next century makes a similar statement. St. Jerome also speaks of the British Pilgrims he had seen in the Holy Land in the fourth century ; British Bishops were present at the Councils of Arles and Rimini in the fourth century, and were invited to the Œcumenical Council of Nicæa, but could not go on account of their poverty. Pieces of Roman pottery with the sacred monogram burnt upon it were found at Padstow. Pelagius a Welshman, in the fourth century, set the whole world in a blaze with his teachings about original sin. These and many other facts make it quite clear that Christianity must have been received by the Celts of Cornwall long before the coming of the so-called Irish Missionaries to Cornwall, to two of whom the districts of Breage and Germoe owe their names.

The Pagan Saxons landed on the east coast of England in the fifth century and drove the Christian Brythons before them, putting all to the sword who fell into their hands. Those who escaped took refuge either in Cornwall, Wales or Brittany. It is from the Celts, therefore, with a strong admixture of Ivernian blood, that the present inhabitants, at any rate of Western Cornwall, are descended. As a result of the Saxon invasion of Britain it came about that Wales and Cornwall were fully Christian, whilst the rest of Britain became practically Pagan. The Venerable Bede, the Anglo-Saxon historian monk of Jarrow, goes so far as to blame the Celts of Cornwall and Wales for altogether neglecting the conversions of the Anglo-Saxons to Christianity. Considering the nature of the case, this was a most unreasonable complaint to make, as the Saxons at once killed or enslaved any Celts unlucky enough to fall into their hands. If further proof were needed that Wales and Cornwall were Christian at this time, we have only to turn to the writings of Gildas* and the Welsh Bards, Taliesin, Aneurin and Llwarch-Hen. The memorials of these writers date from the sixth century and depict incidentally Christianity in a highly organised condition among the Celts of the West.

Leland the antiquarian, who visited Cornwall and consequently Breage in the reign of Henry VIII, amongst other things of interest in the Parishes of Breage and Germoe which he noticed, speaks of the ruins of the ancient Castle or Stone Fort on the summit of Tregoning Hill.   He says : " The Castle of Conan stood on the hill of Pencair, there yet appeareth two ditches, some say that Conan had a son called Tristrame."   The life of the chieftain Conan and all that he did have long since faded into oblivion ; all that survives of him are the mounds of stones that mark the site of his rude stronghold, and his name which has escaped oblivion in the name of the hill on which he lived and ruled—Tregoning, " Tre Conan " the abode or settlement of Conan.   Pencair, the name which Leland gives to Tregoning Hill, merely means the Hill of the Castle or Camp.

The two round camps on the eastern face of Tregoning Hill, formed by the casting up of high banks of earth with a deep ditch on the outer side, are the work of Brythons, or at any rate of people who had adopted their method of fortification and defence ; the Goidels made the breastwork of their camps of stone.   In those lawless days all communities had to fortify themselves against the sudden attacks of enemies, just as, on the north-western frontier of India, all the villages at the present day are fortified against attack by high walls of mud.   The two camps or settlements on Tregoning are well chosen near an excellent water supply and on the side of the hill sheltered from the blustering gales coming up from the sea. Possibly at the time when these two camps were the haunts of two populous communities the whole of the low lying land of Breage and Germoe was covered with swamp, tangled scrub and undergrowth.

The first definite tradition bearing upon the history of the Parish is the arrival of St. Breaca with St. Germoe, somewhere about 500. It is said that they landed at the mouth of the Hayle River in company with between seven and eight hundred Irish Saints, both men and women, who are supposed to have come from the Province of Munster. From the legends that have come down to us with regard to them we gather that they were not altogether wanted by the Cornish. However, this was a minor consideration to such a large band of enthusiastic Irish men and women; they made a forcible landing and drove back the Cornish Chief Teudor and his men who opposed their landing. The legends describe Teudor as a cruel heathen, in which surely there must be some mistake, as Teudor is a Christian name, being only Cornish for Theodore. The legends go on to tell us that one of this great company of Saints, a woman called Cruenna was killed at Crowan in trying to take forcible possession of the land of one who was already a Christian, for the purpose of building a church upon it. It seems very much as if these Irish men and women, with the true impulsiveness, of their race, set out to Cornwall to convert the inhabitants, without first taking the trouble to find out whether or no they were Christians. We see instances of the same spirit at work to-day, Methodist Missionaries in Rome to convert Roman Catholics, and Roman Catholic Missionaries in England to convert Christians who are not Roman Catholics.

It may be helpful, in considering this matter, to take a glance at the condition of the people of the country whence these Missionaries came at the time with which we are dealing. St. Patrick, who owed his knowledge of Christianity to St. Ninian, a Briton, first brought Christianity to

Ireland not more than a hundred years before the arrival of the seven hundred and seventy seven Saints in the Hayle River, whilst, as we have seen, Cornwall had been under Christian influences for several centuries. A candid view of Christianity in Ireland at this time can only lead to the conclusion that it was more than half Pagan. The tonsure of the Priests, or mode of cutting their hair, was exactly the same as that of the Druid* Priests. It was not till the year 804 that Monks and Clergy in Ireland were exempt from bearing arms,* that is three hundred years after the coming of these Saints to Cornwall. Women* were not exempt from fighting in the ranks till 500. In 672 a battle was fought between the rival Monasteries of Clonmacnois and Durrow. In 816 four hundred Monks and Nuns* were slain in a pitched battle between two rival Monasteries. In 700 the Irish Clergy* attended their Synods sword in hand, and fought with those who differed from them on doctrinal points, leaving the ground strewn with corpses. The Irish, no doubt with the wild unreasoning enthusiasm so characteristic of the race, flung themselves into the new movement, and the Monasteries were soon filled with Monks and Nuns with but a vague realisation of what Christianity was ; many no doubt would quickly weary of the new life of rule, and yearn for one of greater variety ; hence possibly the swarming off to other lands in search of spiritual adventures.

The theory has been suggested that our army of Irish Saints were fugitives, worsted in battle, escaping from their enemies, as Ireland at this period was devastated with petty tribal wars. This theory, to say the least, seems most plausible.

Vague traditions have come down to us of incidents in the lives of the Saints of this period which reveal something of the moral atmosphere in which they lived and moved and

---

*See Stokes' "Celtic Church" and Baring Gould's "Lives of the Saints."

had their being. At the end of Germoe Lane there used to be a cairn of great stones, which an ignorant local administration has long since cleared away. The legend of these stones was that St. Keverne possessed a beautiful eucharistic chalice and paten. St. Just the holy visited his friend and stole these sacred vessels. St. Keverne discovered the loss and pelted the flying St. Just with the great stones that fell at the end of Germoe Lane. The same story appears in the life of St. Patrick where the annalist reveals his bias in the words : " O wonderful deed ! O the theft of a treasure of holy things, the plunder of the most holy places of the world !" Straws show the way in which the wind blows, and this fable and the comments of the Irish annalist reveal the view of his age on the question of theft.

Of course, we fully admit that the Irish Monasteries did become for a time the home of the learning of the age such as it was. We do not forget their great foundations in Germany and Northern Italy, and their exquisite skill in the work of illumination as in the books of Durrow and Kells ; what we contend is that the Irish Saints in coming to Cornwall were coming to a land which possessed a Christianity older and purer than their own. That the Irish Saints were sincere according to their lights we do not doubt, and being true to the light they possessed they are worthy of being held in honour.

It has been suggested as a solution for the reason of the Invasion of the Irish Saints, that at the close of the fifth and the beginning of the sixth century Cornwall was only partially christianized, that Pagans and Christians were living side by side in amity, and that the Irish Saints came to devote themselves to the conversion of the Pagans. Whether this solution of the difficulty be true or no, at any rate it is opposed to all that we can gather from the testimony of ancient writers and hagiographers, and, if we accept it, we must reject their testimony as utterly false and worthless.

Of course, a distinction must be made between the Hibernian Saints and the many Saints who came over from Brittany and settled in Cornwall. The people of Brittany were one in language and character with the Cornish to a far greater extent than the Irish ; and, like the Cornish, the people of Brittany had been under Christian influences several centuries before the Irish had.

Amongst the Saints who came from Ireland with Breaca and Germoe was Gwithian, said to have been killed in the fighting with Teudor or Theodore ; Cruenna, killed at Crowan ; Wendron, who made his settlement at Wendron ; Moran, who settled at Madron ; Ia, who settled at St. Ives ; St. Levan, said to have been Breaca's brother, settled at St. Levan ; the names of others also have come down to us whom we need not mention. Germoe is supposed to have been of royal descent, which means that he was related to the petty king or chief of his sept or tribe. Breaca is said in the vague traditions that have come down to us, originally to have pursued the calling of a midwife ; Leland, the great antiquary of the reign of Henry VIII, when he visited Cornwall, saw many legendary lives of the Cornish Saints, from which he made extracts. Most of these lives were destroyed with much else that was beautiful and valuable at the time of the Reformation.

The last book of the lives of our local Saints was in the library of Sir William Howard of Naworth Castle in Cumberland, in the reign of Queen Elizabeth. It was carried thither by a Cornish Roman Priest, who took refuge with him and acted as his Chaplain. This valuable volume has been long lost sight of.*

Amongst other things Leland tells us that when he visited Germoe, St. Germoe's grave was pointed out to him ; of the site of the grave even tradition is now altogether silent ; he

---

*See Borlase's "Age of the Saints."

also mentions having seen St. Germoe's well "a little without the churchyard."

At Breage Leland made some extracts from a life of St. Breaca that was shown to him doubtless by the then Vicar of Breage ; the life in those days would be a very precious possession of our Church. From Leland we gather that Breaca had begun her religious life in a Monastery founded by the famous St. Bridget, Abbess of Kildare ; as to the exact site of this Monastery the statement made by Leland is somewhat vague and difficult.* He goes on to tell us that after the struggle of the Saints with Teudor and his defeat, Breaca first took up her abode at Pencair, that is Tregoning Hill, and built a Church somewhere near Chynoweth and Tolmena on the south eastern slopes of the hill. Of course it is now quite impossible to locate the site of this ancient Church ;† at the best it would be small and poor and the materials of its construction of no durable character. From this spot Leland tells us that Breaca migrated to the site on which our present Church stands, a spot which has been hallowed to the service of God by fifteen hundred years of worship. Generation after generation through the whole course of English history have there lifted up their hearts to God, and generation after generation have been laid to rest under the shadow of its sacred walls on the edge of the hill overlooking the sea. That Breaca settled at Chynoweth is strangely borne out by facts. The two fortified camps previously referred to are contiguous to the spot, and the surrounding

---

*Leland says "Campus Breacae in Hibernia in quo Brigida oratorium construxit et postea Monaster, in quo fuit et S. Breaca." It will be noticed that this statement does not support the view of the Revd. S. Baring Gould that Breaca is a latinised form of Bridget, in his Lives of British Saints. Professor Gwynn of Dublin informs the writer: "Breaca could not possibly be a form of Bridget." In support of this view he quotes Prof. Loth in LaRevue Celtique vol. 29, p. 237 on St. Briac "Ce Saint est donné comme irlandaise ce que semblerait confirmer la terminaison. Il faut supposer une forme irlandaise ' Briacc.'"

†Leland : "Breaca aedificavit ecclesiam in Trenewith et Talmeneth ut legitur in vita St. Elwini."

fields on the slopes of Tregoning hill, bear abundant evidences of having been the site of a considerable settlement in Celtic times ; huge stones that once no doubt did duty in stone avenues and circles have been piled by farmers of a latter age into boundary walls of cyclopean character, whilst the curious may still find ancient querns and stones fashioned to the rude uses of a forgotten age.

In ancient deeds the Church of Breage bears the name of Eglos Pembroc *i.e.* the Church on the Hill of Breaca. The name still lives on in the name Pembro Farm, standing on the same hill.

When Breaca and those who followed her settled on the edge of the hill on which our Church stands and when amicable relationships had been established with those dwelling around, the first thing the Saint would attempt would be the erection of a small Church, built of wattle work, mud and stone. The only relic of that ancient period that still remains is the red sand stone Celtic Cross by the Church

The Celtic Cross in Breage Churchyard.

door, unearthed a few years ago in our churchyard ; this ancient cross must have been brought from a distance, as there is no red sand stone at all near. It is interesting to speculate why it was brought to Breage from some distant place; perhaps it was brought from Ireland, and to Breaca was fraught with memories of a greater and older foundation.

The site which Breaca selected for the building of her Church had been probably the site of ancient heathen worship through many centuries. It seems to have been the custom, wherever possible, for the early founders of Christian Churches to select ancient heathen sites.[*] Their building on these ancient sites was at once symbolical of the victory of the Cross over heathendom, and evidence that the Demons which were supposed to haunt their ancient sanctuaries were powerless against the Saints either to harm or to hinder. The tower of Breage Church from its position is visible far out to sea, and for miles over the surrounding country from every point of the compass but the West. The hill on which it stands, therefore, dominating alike land and sea, is just the spot that the Priests of "a creed outworn" would have selected, at once excellent for astronomical observations and for rivetting the distant gaze of the votaries of their faith.

When this site had been finally selected, a little hut would be erected on the spot, in which Breaca would take up her abode and continue all alone in fasting and prayer for a period of forty days ; during the whole of this time she would eat nothing from sunrise to sunset, except on Sundays, when possibly she might partake of an egg, a morsel of bread with a little milk mixed with water. When the forty days were accomplished all had been done in the way of consecration.[†]

---

[*]See "Byeways of British Archæology" by W. Johnson.—*Cambridge University Press.*

[†] See Bede.

C

The Churches thus built were naturally called after their founders, but as Professor Rhys points out, it remained for a subsequent generation to give them the informal title of Saint. It is well for us to realise that these Cornish Saints were never formally canonized.

We must bear in mind also that in Celtic times there were no Parishes and no Dioceses. The little colonies of the Saints were independent communities ; they kept their own Bishops, who held quite a subordinate position ; at Kildare, St. Bridget had a number of Bishops under her orders, so had Ninnock in Brittany and Columba in Iona. Our conception of a diocese was altogether foreign to the Celtic mind.* Bishops were kept as a species of ecclesiastical Queen Bee. The Saintship or headship of the community was hereditary, descending from father to son. The manner of life of the Saints was rude and barbarous in the extreme. They wore a thick outer garment of wool or of skin, with an inner garment of lighter texture ; on their feet they wore sandals, they slept on hides with a pillow of straw.†

With the foundation of Churches at Breage and Germoe by Breaca and Germoe, thick mist closes in again over the history of the Parish for several hundred years. The communities these two Saints founded would continue to live peacefully in all probability under the rule of their successors until the coming of the time of the Saxon settlement. No doubt at some time during this period of darkness the Church life and administration would come to be organised more and more. on the plan with which we are familiar.

As a line of Cornish Bishops in communion with Canterbury and the rest of the Church gradually asserted their authority, the old rule of the Saints over separate and distinct Christian communities would gradually pass away, and thus

---

* Stokes' "Celtic Church."

† Constitutions of Columba,

the separate atoms would coalesce and become united under one single authority—the Bishop of the Diocese in which their community was settled.

In 813 Egbert, the Saxon King, invaded Cornwall, and marched from one end to the other, spreading fire and sword in his path. In 926 Athelstan, the Saxon King, defeated the Cornish at the battle of Hingeston Down near Calstock. The complete subjugation of Cornwall quickly followed, and with this conquest the soil of our parish would soon pass under the hands of Saxon lords, and the Saxon system of government would quickly supplant altogether the old systems of Celtic times.

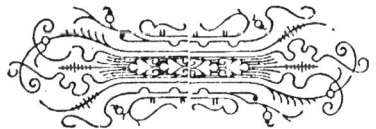

THE SAXONS.

CHAPTER II.

The oldest written documents dealing with the life of the people of Breage in the past are contained in William the Conqueror's Domesday Book. The Domesday Book contains a general survey of all the land in England, which William the Conqueror caused to be made after his usurpation of the English throne in 1066 This book contains the description of four manors in the Parish of Breage, Metela, Rentis, or, as we call them, Methleigh and Rinsey, and the two smaller manors of Tregew and Trescowe. The following is what we read concerning them. " The Bishop has one manor which is called Metela* (Methleigh) which Bishop Leofric held in the time of King Edward, and it rendered tribute for one hide, but yet there is a hide and a half. Fifteen teams can plough this. Thereof the Bishop has half a hide and one plough in demesne, and the villeins one hide and eight ploughs. There the Bishop has fifteen villeins and four bordars and three serfs and three cows and twenty sheep and sixty acres of underwood and forty acres of pasture. Of this manor the Count of Mortain has a yearly market, which Bishop Leofric held in the time of King Edward." " Ulward holds of the Count one manor, which is called Rentis, and therein is one hide of land. Twelve teams can plough this. Ulward and his villeins have there one plough, one cow and thirty sheep, and eight coliberts and four serfs and of pasture half a league in length and the same in breadth." Attached to the manor

---

*This ancient Manor of Methleigh was much bigger than the present estate of Methleigh. It most probably comprised a large portion of the present district of Kenneggie. This conclusion finds interesting support from the names of two fields in Kenneggie, viz. the "Sentry" or "Sanctuary Field" and "Church Field." It may be added that the Manor of Methleigh passed from the Bishops of Exeter to the Dean and Chapter of Exeter, and by them was alienated from the Church.

of Rentis or Rinsey the Count of Mortain had in demesne a quarter of a hide of land ; this portion was probably tilled by the Count's steward or agent. " The Count has a manor which is called Trescowe, which Alnod held in the time of King Edward and still holds of the Count, and it paid tribute for the $\frac{1}{16}$ of a hide. Three teams can plough this. Thereof Alnod has $\frac{1}{48}$ part of a hide in demesne, and the villeins the remaining land and one plough. There Alnod has three bordars and one serf and three acres of wood and 100 acres of pasture." " The Count has one manor which is called Tregew, which Brismar held in the time of King Edward. There is one quarter of a hide of land and it paid tribute for $\frac{1}{16}$ of a hide. Three teams can plough this. Heldric holds this of the Earl, and has in demesne $\frac{1}{32}$ of a hide and one plough, and the villeins have the remaining land and one plough. There Heldric has six bordars and two serfs and forty sheep and forty acres of pasture."

The manors were grants of land made by the king to noblemen, or as they were then called thanes. As a return for this gift of land the thane had to go to the wars with the king and fight for him when the king desired his services, and also he had to give assistance in the building of the king's castles and strongholds. The land on a Saxon manor was dealt with in two ways ; part of it was held and culti-vated by the thane himself, this was called demesne land, and the other portion of it was cultivated by the thane's tenants, who were called villeins. The villein would usually hold a strip of land called a virgate, possibly equal to about thirty acres. The thane provided him with two oxen and one cow and seed sufficient for seven acres of land for each of the thirty acres or virgates that he held. The villein or tenant was not a free man and could not leave the manor without the consent of his lord, and in transfers of manors the villeins passed with the land. They paid tribute to their lord both in money and in the produce of the land they cultivated; also on certain days in each week, according to the season, they had to give their labour free on the land cultivated by the lord or thane. Below these larger villein holders came a class called coliberts, cottars or bordars, who held about five acres of land each. These inferior tenants had to work for their lord without wage on each Monday throughout the year and three days each week during the period of harvest. Below these again were the serfs who worked on their lord's demesne; they were slaves bought and sold in the market and often exported from English ports across the sea as part of the commercial produce of the country. Most of us are familiar with the story of Pope Gregory the Great, who, walking in the Roman slave-market, saw a number of fair-haired Saxon slave boys exposed for sale, and who, seeing these children, vowed to do his best for the conversion of their country to Christianity. On the Breage manors it is more than probable that the slaves would not be Saxons but Celts. Many of the manor slaves were slaves from birth, but it also seems not to have been an uncommon practice for free men to sell themselves into slavery under the pressure of want.

The cultivated land round each ancient Saxon manor village was marked off according to the custom of the time into three enormous unfenced fields. Each householder in the village above the rank of slave had a greater or less number of strips or shares in each of these three fields. When the time for ploughing came round, as no villager possessed a team of eight oxen—the number required to draw the primitive Saxon plough—the team for the general ploughing was contributed jointly by the villagers. The advantage of this system will therefore be obvious. Custom decreed further that each year one of these great open fields held in strips by the villagers should lie fallow; that another of them should be sown with oats or rye; and a third should be sown down with barley. Some of this last crop would be used for bread, but we fear that a great deal of it would be devoted to drink, for the Saxons were men who loved to drink themselves drunk, probably ascribing the ill effects of the beer, enhanced no doubt by the relaxing climate, to anything but the right cause. Not content with a large supply of beer, the Saxons impressed the honey bee into the service of Bacchus, and manufactured from honey great quantities of mead. It is probable that in a seaboard parish like Breage, fish would be a staple article of diet; from the smallness of the number of live stock on the manors, flesh can only have been a rare article of diet, possibly enjoyed by the bounty of the lord of the manor on the great festivals of the Church.*

The vast mass of the country at this period was wild, uncultivated and uninhabited. Such would be the condition of the greater part of the Parish of Breage in Saxon times. The valleys would be filled with a thick undergrowth, their beds forming impassable swamps, whilst the higher ground would be more or less covered with furze and scrub, in which wolves would make their lairs, preying upon the flocks and from time to time carrying off a child that had strayed too far from the parental hut of clay.

The land measure called a hide made use of in the Domesday record is supposed to have contained 120 acres;† a virgate was the term used for a quarter of a hide or thirty acres. The virgate was again divided into quarters, called ferlings, of 7½ acres each. We must not confound this word ferling with our present word "furlong," which originally meant the longest furrow which it was deemed possible a team of oxen could plough without stopping, viz., 220 yards.

Unfortunately Domesday is silent with regard to mining matters, and consequently we can gather nothing as to the nature of the mining carried on in our Parish in Saxon

---

*For the conditions of life on Anglo-Saxon Manor see Seebohm's "Village Communities."
† The exact size of the ancient Cornish acre is unknown.

times. There can be no doubt that mining of an elementary character was carried on, but of its extent and the number of those engaged in it, it would be rash to theorise. Knowing nothing therefore of the number of the population engaged in mining we can form no approximate estimate of the local population, but at any rate we may conclude that it cannot have been great. The bordars and slaves mentioned on the four manors only come to twenty-eight; on the largest of the manors, Metela or Methleigh, there were fifteen villeins; the number of villeins on the other three manors is not stated—simply the fact that there were villeins; but as Methleigh was about the size of the other three manors put together we may conclude these manors also possessed in all about fifteen villeins. This would give us a total of sixty-one villeins, bordars and serfs enumerated; if we multiply this number by five for the women and children of their respective families, it gives us a total agricultural population for the parishes of Breage and Germoe of three hundred and five, with eighteen teams of oxen, four cows, and ninety sheep. It is interesting to notice that the live stock were enumerated before the slaves, presumably because they were the more valuable.

The houses or huts in which the Cornish villeins, bordars and serfs lived on the Saxon manors would be composed of clay, with a hole in the roof to let the smoke out; their inhabitants from constantly sitting in the smoke suffered greatly from diseases of the eyes; of sanitation there was none, and human life was exceedingly short. This condition of things practically continued in Cornwall to the end of the Tudor period as we gather from the picture of Cornish life given to us by Carew in his "Survey of Cornwall" written in the reign of Elizabeth.

Compelled by law to live on the manor on which they were born and to give a great part of their labour free to their lord, the lives of the ancient inhabitants of Breage, judged at any rate by our standards, must have been dull and hard indeed.

Each manor had its own court for the trial of cases which concerned only persons living on the manor ; this court was under the presidency of the baron or thane, assisted by ten freemen. Where the freemen were not to be found, as in our Breage manors, cases were tried by the Court cf the Hundred in which the manor was situated. The Court of the Hundred also tried suits in the case of the larger manors which involved people living in two or more different manors.*

From the legal view of things we naturally pass to matters ecclesiastical. In approaching this view of the life of our parish in Saxon times it is interesting in the first place to note that the Manor of Rinsey formed part of the great Manor and Hundred of Winnington, which comprised a large portion of the Lizard district, including Cury and Gunwalloe. We have here a hint as to the reason why Breage, Cury and Gunwalloe have always been ecclesiastically one until recent times, as roughly they formed a considerable part of the Hundred of Winnington. It was natural that this large Manor should be regarded as an ecclesiastical unit. We find this unity complete in the earliest extant ecclesiastical document, dated 1219, given in the Patent Rolls, and it seems natural to conclude that this unity dates from the foundation of the Saxon Manor. Breage was an †" ecclesia," Cury and Gunwalloe were " Capellæ " in the *Inquisitio Nonarum* of 1346 ; in other words there was only one parish with several chapelries. Most probably in the Saxon period the collegiate system prevailed in our part of Cornwall, and

---

*Inderwick's "The King's Peace."

It is fair to add that the Rev. T. Taylor informs me :—"An examination of the Court Rolls given by Maitland makes it evident that where there were few freemen, the villeins were suitors at the Court, and that it is impossible to say that the absence of the former drove the villeins to the Hundred Court."

†In the *Inquisitio Nonarum* of 1346 the phrase "ecclesia Sanctae Bryacae cum capellis Sanctorum Correnti Wynyantoni et Gyrmough" occurs.

Breage may have performed for the western half of the Meneage Peninsula what St. Keverne did for the eastern half. We find mention of the Canons of St. Keverne, but there is no record of the Canons of Breage.

The Bishop Leofric referred to in the account of the Manor of Methleigh became first Bishop of Cornwall and Crediton in 1046 ; in the same year the title of the See was changed, and Leofric became the first Bishop of Exeter. Possibly the Manor of Methleigh, which thus passed to the See of Exeter, had originally been a portion of the settlement of Breaca which had passed to the Bishops of Bodmin or St. Germans on the reorganization of the Church in Saxon times on continental lines. There had been Cornish Bishops in full communion with the See of Canterbury from 865, governing their Sees from either Bodmin or St. Germans.

The Earl or Count mentioned in the extracts from Domesday was Robert, Earl of Cornwall, and Count of Mortain in Normandy. He was the bastard half-brother of William the Conqueror. The Earls of Cornwall to all intents and purposes within the bounds of the earldom were reigning princes. The earldom was not hereditary ; a special creation took place at the death of each Earl, or in case of the earldom having been forfeited through rebellion. Earl Robert obtained enormous spoils from his half-brother William on his conquest of England ; some idea of the plunder thus obtained may be gathered from the fact that in Domesday we find him possessed of 797 manors in various counties.

After this brief record of our Parish and its Manors to be found in Domesday, its history is again utterly lost in impenetrable obscurity for 250 years, when documents, especially of an ecclesiastical nature, became more frequent, and the main outline of its story becomes much clearer.

From the Norman Conquest to the Reformation.

CHAPTER III.

In dealing with the Norman period, to make the story of Breage clear, it is necessary in the first place again to refer briefly to the Earldom of Cornwall. From the time of the Norman Conquest, when the earldom was created, to the time of Edward the Black Prince, when it was exalted into a duchy, the earldom was held by a series of twelve earls. Since the time of the Black Prince the Duchy of Cornwall has always been held by the eldest son of the reigning Sovereign.

Giraldus describes the ecclesiastical polity of the Normans in no flattering terms. If his version be correct—and there seems little reason in the main to doubt it—the Normans simply regarded the endowments of the Church as a means of satisfying the rapacity of a swarm of needy ecclesiastics from the other side of the Channel.

As the possession of the land was torn from the Saxon nobles and handed over as largess to Norman Knights, so too the endowments of the Church were regarded as fitting spoil for Norman Priests. According to Giraldus, the method of the Norman Priest might be summed up in the words "*pasci non pascere.*" He also charges the Norman Clergy with great ignorance and gross immorality, though many of the Saxon Clergy were dispossessed by the Conqueror on the specious charge of immorality, as the Prior and Canons of Plympton St. Mary, near Plymouth. Doubtless the invectives of Giraldus are somewhat highly coloured, but after all it seems but too clear that they contain more than a substratum of truth.

It is evident from existing remains that Norman Churches

were built both at Breage and Germoe, possibly about the year 1100. The building of these Churches was no doubt at the expense of the Earls of Cornwall, in accordance with the prevailing custom. Whether Saxon Churches succeeded the ancient Celtic Churches it is impossible to say. If the Saxons did find the humble Celtic Churches inadequate and built new ones, at any rate no vestige or record of them survives. The remains of the Norman Church built on the site of the present Church at Breage consist only of a couple of fragments, but yet these two fragments are sufficient to make it clear that the present Church was preceded by a Norman Church. A projecting stone of bluish grey colour, let into the northern wall by the door of the present vestry, bears distinct marks of Norman workmanship, and some twenty years ago more than a fragment of a Norman font was found outside the north door of our Church. This interesting relic was incorporated into the new font at present in use, which was fashioned on the model of the ancient Norman font at Cury.

At Germoe, on the other hand, the remains of a Norman Church are altogether more abundant. Here the foundations and lower portions of the east and south walls are evidently of Norman workmanship, as also the east and south walls of the south transept. During the restoration of 1891 the head of a Norman window was discovered built into the wall of the south transept. This little window has been carefully restored by the addition of two new jambs and a stone sill; on examination it will be discovered that this Norman window arch is slightly chamfered. Other discoveries made at the restoration were the Norman corbel heads, now built into the outside face of the east wall of the north aisle, and the bowl of a Norman stoup, which has been built into the south wall of the nave, with a new arch placed over it. In the foundations of the Church was also discovered the bowl of a mutilated Norman font, which now stands on a new rough-hewn stem in the north transept. The date of this font is placed by Mr. Sedding, in his "Norman Churches in Cornwall," at about 1100. If we regard this date of 1100 as correct, it will serve as some clue to the date of the building of the Norman Churches at Breage and Germoe. Assuming this date to be approximately correct, the churches were built by William Fitz Robert or William de Mortain, Earl of Cornwall, son of Earl Robert de Mortain of Domesday Book. This unfortunate nobleman joined his cousin Robert de Belesme in rebellion against Henry I. with disastrous consequences. He was taken prisoner at the battle of Tenchebrai and deprived of his estates and honours, and his eyes were put out by the hands of the executioner. In his blindness and misery he sought peace in the bosom of the Church, of which it seems at least probable that he was a benefactor in the days of his prosperity, and died a Cluniac Monk in the Monastery of Bermondsey.

The question of patronage is one of extreme difficulty ; it seems more than probable that the patronage went to the builders of the Churches ; in this case the patronage of Breage would naturally pass at the building of the Norman Churches to the Earldom of Cornwall. At any rate we find the patronage of the benefice attached to the Earldom at the beginning of the thirteenth century.

Leland states that Germoe was originally a cell of St. Michael's Mount. In this statement he is followed by Hals. It seems probable that on this point Leland was misled by some statement made locally to him, as there is no shred of existing evidence to support this view. Domesday and the Monasticon are alike silent upon the subject and lend no countenance to it. It is true Hals, apparently in support of this contention, evolved a fictitious Inquisition of the Bishops of Winchester and Gloucester from the depths of his subliminal consciousness. In this precious Inquisition " Sancto Gordon," as Germoe is styled " in the Deanery of

Kerrier," is valued at £8. More to the point is the fact that in 1246 Richard, Earl of Cornwall, made over the living of Breage with the Chapels of Cury, Gunwalloe and Germoe to the Abbey of Hayles.

In Lysons' Cornwall it is stated that the Chapel of St. Germoe was given by William, Earl of Gloucester, to the Priory of St. James, Bristol. The learned authors have here fallen into a mistake for which there is reasonable excuse ; they have confounded the church of St. Breoke* in North Cornwall with St. Breage and a Church of Germot, possibly on the Norman lands of the Earl of Gloucester, with Germoe. The Earl of Gloucester never held any lands in this district. This statement of the Lysons has also been freely used by subsequent writers of county histories. It seems clear that at no period of its history was Germoe ever ecclesiastically independent of Breage ; it is probable that in early times it was served like Cury and Gunwalloe by clergy living together under the collegiate system at Breage. In the *Inquisitio Nonarum* of 1346 we read " ecclesia Sanctae Bryacae cum Capellis Sanctorum Corenti, Wynyantoni et Gyrmough," which makes it quite clear that at that date Germoe was included in the parish of Breage.

With the coming of the Normans the value of Cornwall's mineral wealth seems to have been quickly grasped. The successive Earls were greedy foreigners, who valued their Fief mainly for what it would produce; it was not so much Cornwall they wanted as Cornwall's wealth. By the time of Richard, Earl of Cornwall, King of the Romans, the mines of Cornwall had become a source of immense wealth, 1224-72 Possibly the building of Churches both at Breage and Germoe in Norman times may have been due

---

* "Carta W. Com. Glouc testificante quod R. Com. pater suus dederat Richardo Clerico suo omnes ecclesias terrae suae de Cornubia cum capellis et pertinentis suis viz: ecclesiam de Eglosbrec. ecclesiam Commart, ecclesiam de Egloshiel, ecclesiam de Eglosvant, ecclesiam de Eglosccraven et capellam Sancti Germot" etc., etc. See Dugdale's Monasticon.

to the large influx of population owing to the opening up of local mines.

At the beginning of the Norman period the people of Breage were living under the ordinary Manorial and King's Courts, but very soon all this was changed by the Norman Earls in their policy of mine development, and the rule of the Stannary Courts was added. By the Charter of 1201, Stannary Courts were set up which held civil and criminal jurisdiction over the Miners or Tinners, as they were called. A Stannary Parliament, consisting of twenty-four Senators, met at Hingston Down, near Calstock, and chose a Speaker of its own ; subsequently this Parliament for the government of the Miners and the regulation of mining affairs seems to have met at Truro. The Stannaries were divided into five districts, of which Penwith and Kerrier formed one. The Cornish Miners thus came to be formed into a little State by themselves ; they paid no taxes to the King but to the Stannaries, and these they paid not as Englishmen but as Miners, Their Parliament was the mine Parliament, their Courts were the mine Courts. The influence of this state of things was in the main bad ; it gave opportunity for the oppression and consequent debasement of the Miners, and tended to make the people lawless and impatient of all restraint. Long after this ancient system had passed away its evil fruits remained in a certain lawlessness of disposition. Carew, writing in the days of Queen Elizabeth, remarks that it was a matter of notoriety in his day that the mining districts of Cornwall were farthest behind the general level of culture. The reason of this we take to be due, to a large extent, to the lawlessness, abuses and evils engendered by the Stannary Courts, which at one and the same time placed the mining population above the law and beyond the arm of its protection.

The following letter of King Henry III., written in 1219 to Simon de Apulia, an Italian Bishop of Exeter, referring to the living of Breage, which is given in the Patent Rolls, is of interest. The two Vicars of Breage mentioned in this document are the earliest of whom we have any record.

" The King to Simon, Bishop of Exeter, greeting ; be it known that on the resignation of William the son of Richard, Parson of the Churches of Eglospenbroc, Egloscure and Winiton now deceased, i.e. the Churches of Breage, Cury and Gunwalloe, Our Lord King John conferred the said Churches on our beloved Clerk, William, the son of Humphrey, the aforesaid Churches being in his appointment. But since the same William was prevented from following his claim on account of the disturbed state of the time, we now send him to your fatherly care, asking you to admit no one else to those Churches contrary to the gift already made by the King our Father, but to kindly institute the said William, showing yourself kindly disposed in this matter for love of us." This document under the specious phrase " disturbed state of the times " evidently refers to the period of the Interdict which had only come to a close some five years previously— a period when by the insensate wickedness of King and Pope the whole apparatus of the religious life of the country was thrown out of gear and ceased to perform its functions, to the infinite sorrow and misery of many thousands of the people.

In 1246 Richard, Earl of Cornwall, King of the Romans, made over the Church of Breage with the Chapelries of Cury, Gunwalloe and Germoe to the Abbey of St. Mary, at Hayles in Worcestershire. The story of this Prince reads more like a romance than a record of sober fact. He was the second son of King John. Born in 1209, Richard was made a Knight and Earl of Cornwall at the early age of sixteen. Before his seventeenth birthday he had shewn himself to be a fearless soldier in the wars of Gascony. Three years later he took the field again against the French King, this time in the North of France. The campaign was barren of all results, but memorable for the terrible slaughter of its battles and the ruin and misery wrought upon the poor peasants of the country in which it was waged, who knew less than nothing at all as to what it was all about. In this terrible campaign Richard lost his friend Gilbert De Clare, Earl of Gloucester. Richard consoled himself for the loss of his friend by marrying his widow, whose beauty and golden tresses the old chronicler delights to dwell upon.

This warlike brother of an unwarlike king bitterly inveighed against the royal favourites who battened upon the wealth of the nation. "England has become a vineyard without a wall, wherein all who pass by pluck off her grapes," he exclaimed.

In 1241 we find Richard at Rome endeavouring to mediate between Pope Gregory IX. and his mighty brother-in-law the Emperor Frederick IL, "Stupor Mundi," the most gifted sovereign of his age, if not of any age. The Pope was practically the Emperor's prisoner at Grotto Ferrata, and during the terrible August heat, which was accompanied by pestilence, Richard passed to and fro between Pope and Emperor. At length the negotiations were put an end to by death claiming the aged Pontiff.

His beautiful wife Isabella de Clare died at an early age, and Richard with a sad heart went off to the Crusades, where, by liberal largess, wrung from the serfs of his fiefs no doubt, rather than by the sword, we read he was able to open the gates of Jerusalem and raise the banner of the Cross over Nazareth and Bethlehem.

Returning from the Holy Land, the ship in which he sailed was beset by a terrible storm. In the hour of extreme danger Earl Richard made a vow to the Virgin that, if by the mercy of God the ship was saved from the storm, he would build a great abbey to her honour and richly endow it.

On his return, in obedience to his vow, he set about the founding of Hayles Abbey in Worcestershire on a princely scale, to which we have seen he made over the Church of Breage with its three Chapelries. The Church of this Abbey was of the same dimensions as those of Gloucester Cathedral; it was consecrated in 1251 amidst a scene of the greatest splendour, the King and Queen with the majority of the Bishops and many Barons being present. Now only a heap of grass-grown ruins marks the site of this great foundation.

It was in the days of Earl Richard that the tin mines of Cornwall came to be developed on a large scale, and they became to him a source of immense wealth—in fact, a golden key by which he was able to unlock the doors of attainment both in Palestine and Germany. We gather that this Earl was most kindly disposed towards the Jewish race, which assertion lends colour to the statement of Carew that the tin trade of Cornwall in ancient times was largely in the hands of Jews, who grievously exploited the Cornish Tinners.

In 1257 Richard was chosen King of the Romans after the payment of immense bribes to a number of the electing Princes. He returned to England after two years of fruitless war to maintain his shadowy kingdom. He commanded a wing of the Royal Army at the battles of Lewes; on the rout of the royal forces he hid himself in a windmill, from which he was ignominiously dragged and sent a prisoner to the Tower of London. He was released in 1257, and on his death in 1265 his body was laid in the great Abbey which he had founded.

His son, Edmund, succeeded him as Earl of Cornwall; this Prince presented to the Abbey of Hayles one of the most famous relics of the Middle Ages, a reputed phial of the Blood of Christ. This revered relic was kept in a shrine of great magnificence. A curious and interesting report was made on the nature of this supposed relic by the King's Commissioners at the time of the Reformation.*

---

*See Gasquet's "Henry VIII. and the Monasteries."

We have a practically complete list of the Vicars of Breage from the appointment of William, son of Humphrey in succession to William, son of John, in 1219. In the deed already quoted, William, son of Richard, is described as the Parson of Breage; this means he was the Rector of the Parish in the full sense of the word. With the grant of the Church of Breage with its three Chapelries to the Abbey of Hayles the day of the Rectors of Breage was over.

The Abbey of Hayles now stood in the place of Rector, and the Abbot appointed a Vicar or substitute in his room, who acted as the deputy of the Abbot and Convent in the parish. The first of the Vicars was Master Robert de la More, who, as well as his two next successors, was appointed by the Bishop, *jure devoluto*; the Abbot of Hayles finding it difficult no doubt to fill up such a distant and remote appointment. Robert de la More seems to have been a person of note in his day.* He was only Vicar of Breage for three months; he subsequently became a Canon of Glasney, an ancient Collegiate foundation near Penryn. In 1276 he was Vicar of Yeovil, and of sufficient importance for the King to address a letter to him with reference to the raising of a loan for the carrying on of the Scottish Campaign. Of his successor, Master Stephanus de Arbor, we are able to gather no particulars, though the figure of his immediate successor, Sir Pascasius rises clear and distinct for a moment out of the mists of the past. It may be well here to remark that the prefix "Master" meant one who had taken the degree of Master of Arts at either of the Universities of Oxford or Cambridge. "Sir," on the contrary, was a title given to those who had studied at the Universities but who had not taken their Master's degree; this we fancy would in the main be due to poverty rather than laziness or lack of ability, as a Master's

---

*See Mr. Thurstan Peter's " Collegiate Church of Glasney."

degree in those days entailed a longer period of residence at the Universities than now. We may conclude that Sir Pascasius was a Cornishman and a member of the clan Pascoe. His name survives in the archives of the Bishops of Exeter, embalmed in a document dated July 1310, which gives a lurid picture of the brutal methods of the age. The Chapel of Buryan was the King's Peculiar, and, as such, was outside the jurisdiction of the Bishop. It was held by Dean and Canons of its own. A dispute had long been simmering between the Dean and the Bishop of Exeter as to the appointment of one John de Beaupré as Canon of Buryan, the Dean refusing to admit him. As a step in this long dispute it seems that Bishop Walter de Stapleton must have issued a commission to certain clergy, possibly for the purpose of instituting John de Beaupré to the vacant canonry in the Chapel of Buryan. The commission was composed, amongst others, of Sir Pascasius, the vicar of Breage, the vicars of St. Keverne, Constantine, St. Erth, Sithney, Grade and Landewednack. Dean Matthew, in seeking redress through the King's Court, complained that when this posse of Clergy arrived at Buryan and found the doors of the Church barred, they proceeded to heap abuse upon him of the most untoward character, and then, having retired, they returned with a battering ram and broke in the doors of the Church, proceeding most unmercifully to beat the defenders of the door in the hour of victory, and, in the case of one of the Dean's servants, to have danced upon his prostrate body so that his life was despaired of. Having thus celebrated their victory they proceeded to exercise jurisdiction* in the Chapel. For this wild assertion, presumably of episcopal authority, they were all heavily fined.

Shortly after this event Bishop Stapleton pronounced Pascasius to be old, blind and infirm, and appointed Master

---

*See Prebendary Hingeston-Randolph's Registers of Bishop Stapleton. "Et in ea jurisdiccionem ordinariam exercere et alia diversa in hac parte attemptare presumpserunt."

Benedict de Arundelle, Professor of Canon Law, his coadjutor. This coadjutor was a scion of the ancient family of
Arundell of Lanherne; he afterwards became Provost of
Glasney, which office he ultimately resigned whilst still remaining one of the Canons of that Foundation till the time
of his death. In addition to his Canonry of Glasney, he
also held the Rectory of Phillack, the patronage of which was
then vested in the Arundell family. Whilst speaking of
Glasney we may add that a third Vicar of Breage, Sir William
Pers, 1466 became a Canon of that ancient house.

The first Vicar of Breage appointed by the Abbot and
Convent of Hayles was David de Lyspein in 1313. The
name of this man makes it clear that he was a foreigner, most
probably a Gascon ; possibly a more correct rendering of his
name would have been David de L'Espagne or David of Spain.
Froissart in his Chronicles has a good deal to say of a gallant
Gascon Knight, Roger d'Espaign, famous for his strength and
valour, who dwelt at the Court of the Count de Foix. Though
these two names are spelt somewhat differently they are practically one and the same, as in the fourteenth century it was
usual to find proper names continually spelt in different ways.
At this time Gascony was a fief of the English Crown, and our
Kings, Bishops and Nobles were continually passing between
the two lands on missions of government, diplomacy or war,
and numbers of Gascon Clergy found their way in their
trains to our shores. It may well have been that David de
Lyspein was one of these.

Sir Pascasius, whatever else he may have been, was a
Pascoe, and a Cornishman. It was one thing to pay tithes to
a Cornishman who was moreover the actual *Persona* of the
parish, and another thing to pay tithes to the Abbot and
Convent of Hayles, of whom no Cornishman knew anything,
and whose representative or vicar was a foreigner, possibly
barely able to speak the English language, let alone the Cornish
tongue, and knowing nothing of the ways or habits of the

people.   England at this period was overrun with French, Italian and Spanish Clergy, and the whole of our Western diocese was in a state of ferment at having foreign clergy thrust into the parishes.   At Yealmpton, in S. Devon, the French vicar thrust upon the people, on the day of his institution, had to fly from the church with the Archdeacon and his retinue, in momentary danger of being "detruncated."   At Tavistock and Plymouth similar assaults were perpetrated upon foreign clergy forced upon the people.

In 1339 a brief was issued by the King to Bishop Grandisson, who himself was a Swiss noble, born on the Lake of Geneva, commanding him to certify what dignities, prebends and other ecclesiastical benefices were held by foreigners in the Diocese of Exeter.

Taking all these circumstances into consideration it would have been surprising if David de Lyspein had had a good time amongst his Cornish parishioners.   The few documents that have come down to us all accentuate the fact that they gave him a rather poor time.   In the registers of Bishop Grandisson we gather from a document bearing date 1335 that at some time previous, he, together with Brother Thomas, a Monk of Hayle, and Proctor of his Convent, had been grievously wounded by Henry de Pengersick, a man of position. No doubt the affray had occurred in an attempt to collect tithe or other dues.   In proceeding to forcible resistance Henry de Pengersick was but carrying into effect the popular sentiment, so strong at this time practically throughout the whole of England.   It is interesting to note that this armed resistance came from an owner of Pengersick.   A tradition of the lawlessness and wild deeds of the owners of Pengersick has been handed down to the present time amongst the country people of the district, and like most traditions seems based on truth.   Judging from the fierce attack on David de Lyspein, or David of Spain, and Brother Thomas, the Militons, who came after, in their wild deeds were but following in the footsteps of those who had gone before. The greater excommunication was placed upon Henry de Pengersick, but as the wounds inflicted did not permanently prevent the two clergy from performing the duties of their office, it was removed on the' payment of due damages. However, matters do not seem to have mended much; in 1337 a decree was issued* granting protection to the Abbot and Convent of Hayles, "who were grievously hindered in receiving the fruits and profits of St. Breaca in Kerrier by persons who threaten and assault their servants and carry away the goods of the Abbey." The people were evidently of opinion that paying tithes to a Worcestershire Convent and a foreigner Vicar was beyond all reason. We see going on in this remote Cornish Parish that which was taking place all over the country, alienating the Church from the hearts of the people, and preparing the way for the great upheaval of the Reformation. No doubt the heart of poor David de Lyspein in the gloom of the Cornish mists and rain, as the Atlantic tempests howled round his rude tenement, yearned for the forest-clad hills of the sunny South, the scent of the pines and the view of the far-off ranges capped with eternal snow that separated his land from Spain. Cornwall was then rude, barbarous and remote, whilst Gascony was softened and humanized with Provençal culture and light.

In 1340 an event occurred which showed that in spite of strained relationships, clergy and people could at times make common cause in a common enterprise. A tradition of the eighteenth century still lingers at Germoe of a clergyman rushing from the pulpit demanding fair play to participate in the spoil of the wreck which the sea was bearing in upon Praa Sands. If this tale be not mythical, this clergyman had at any rate fourteenth century precedent for his action. In 1340 an Irish ship came ashore at Porth-

---

*Patent Rolls.

leven, when sixty-one persons, including several " religious," i.e. persons in orders of religion, broke up the vessel into pieces and carried away the cargo.*

It is not fair to judge the whole life of the community by cases coming before the Courts, but still these cases are sufficiently frequent to bring home to us the utter lawlessness and violence of the times. When we compare the religious life of the fourteenth century as revealed in the State Papers and the Episcopal and Chapter Records with the outlook and condition of the Church to-day, in spite of dark streaks across the horizon of the future, we cannot but be conscious of a wonderful progress, and an exchanging of crude materialism and superstition for high and noble ideals.

The greatest event in its consequences and at the same time the most terrible in the story of the period between the Norman Conquest and the Reformation is the visitation of the Plague or Black Death. The Plague seems to have reached England in 1348 ; it spread from Dorsetshire to London in the November of that year. In the Eastern Counties whole districts were depopulated by this terrible scourge ; and magnificent Churches in remote and lonely parishes still attest the large populations that dwelt around them and gathered in them for worship before the coming of the Black Death.

In our own immediate neighbourhood, at Bodmin alone 1,500 persons died in the terrible visitation. The Clergy seem to have been the greatest sufferers of all, partly no doubt due to their office bringing them in close contact with the dying, and partly no doubt due to the confusion between dirt and holiness that subsisted in the mediæval mind. To realise the awful mortality in the West amongst the Clergy at this period it is only necessary to go over the endless lists of institutions in the Registers of Bishop Gran-

---

*State Papers, 14 Edward III.

disson ; not seldom three institutions to one parish occur in the course of a single year. As a country engaged in a long and desperate war is glad almost to accept recruits of any kind in its closing stages, so the Church, as this awful epidemic proceeded, accepted recruits for the army of God she would have scorned in its beginning. The result of this acceptation was altogether bad ; her influence began to wane, and she lost touch with the life of the people.

Slowly but gradually the black shadow moved westwards extending itself over the County, leaving in its track half-peopled villages and the survivors dwelling under the shadow of an awful and nameless dread. In the extreme West of the County the ravages of the pestilence seem to have been specially terrible in 1362. It seems more than probable that Sir William Pellour, one of our Vicars of Breage, died of it in this year. Bereft in many cases of the majority of those they loved, and with a vision of death and mortality in its most horrible forms graven upon their minds, the view of life of the mass of the people became utterly changed, and this naturally reflected itself upon the whole religious outlook of the time.

Another subtle and deep influence was beginning to stir at this period, even in the remote wilds of Cornwall. On the Continent, in Italy especially, the human mind in the previous century had begun to awake from the torpor and lethargy of a thousand years. The thirteenth century was a glorious springtime of the human soul, when art, philosophy and the desire to know, came back to the human mind. This tide of new life and light in the fourteenth century began to throb and move, even in the remote backwaters of English life, filling the minds of the people with vague yearnings after better things, and producing a condition of deep spiritual dissatisfaction. This spirit found some expression in the great number of Oratories in the leading private houses, that were licensed, all over the Western Diocese. At this time here in Breage, we read that on 2nd Dec. 1398, John Rynsy of Godolghan, and Elinora, his wife, obtained a licence from Bishop Stafford, for Oratories both at Rynsy and Godolghan, with the stipulation that on Sundays and other Feasts they should resort to their Parish Church, whenever it was conveniently possible for them to do so. Again on 6th September 1400, John Pengersick and Joan, his wife, obtained from Bishop Stafford, a licence for a third Oratory in the Parish at their mansion of Pengersick.

Whilst the gentry were making provision for regular worship in their own houses, new Parish Churches were being built in almost every parish. Practically nine-tenths of the Parish Churches in Devon and Cornwall are the product of this age. The people were seeking to express in stone the new ideal that was moving in their minds, and which was destined to find fuller and deeper expression in the Reformation.

Our Churches of Breage and Germoe we owe to this wonderful quickening of religious life in the fourteenth and fifteenth centuries. The old Norman Church at Breage was pulled down in the fifteenth century as inadequate and unworthy, and the present cruciform Church, with its tower sixty-six feet in height, of beautiful workmanship and restful proportions, reared in its place. The Church outwardly to-day is very much as the fifteenth century builders left it. The tiny transepts, which, like the beautiful south porch, externally suggest small battlemented towers, were evidently originally used as side chapels. The frescos with which the whole of the interior walls were once covered, were doubtless painted shortly after the building of the Church.

Fresco painting is the oldest of the arts, its crude beginnings reaching back to the days when palæolithic man sought to exercise it upon the walls of the caverns of the Dordogne. In Egypt the ancient monuments bear witness to its existence from the remotest antiquity. The Etruscans seem to have brought the art with them from the East to Italy, which became in future ages its true home, and where it attained to its highest perfection and beauty. The Romans, probably owing to Greek influences, carried the art much farther than the Etruscans had done. Revived in Italy in the thirteenth, the art reached its highest perfection in the fifteenth century. From Italy the fashion of mural painting spread, and by the fifteenth century seems to have become common even in Cornwall, judging by the records of the survival of numerous fragments. Our frescos were probably painted very soon

Frescos of St. Christopher and Our Lord in Breage Church.

after the building of the Church, in the latter half of the fifteenth century. An important fact bearing upon fresco painting was the extreme rapidity with which the work had to be accomplished, as the secret of its permanency rested in the plaster upon which it was placed, being damp and newly laid. It will strike the observer at Breage that the fresco of St. Christopher and that of the Christ, though crude in execution, are full of character and force, which the wooden and purely conventional figures of the other frescos entirely lack. It seems evident therefore that the former owe their origin to a different hand than the latter.

The fresco of St. Christopher arrests the eye immediately on entering the Church through the south door. This was doubtless the intention of the designer of the fresco, as to see St. Christopher on entering a Church, according to mediæval superstition was a harbinger of good luck. This may partly account for the superstition that still lingers, that to enter the Church by the west door, which is never used, save for the bearing out of the dead at funerals, foreshadows untimely death.

The windows of the Church, before the pillage and vandalism let loose upon it by the Reformation, were all of stained glass, of which several beautiful fragments have come down to us, as the head of St. Veronica in the chapel at the end of the north aisle, and the heads of the two angels in the south window of the chapel, on the south side of the Church. The Reformation, like all great upheavals, beneficent in themselves, led to the unchaining of the spirit of fanaticism and rapine. The spirit of liberty was fanned into a flame in France before the Revolution by the noblest and purest spirits in the country ; yet who could blame them for the frenzied orgies of the Terror ? The few fragments of fifteenth century glass were discovered with the bones and skulls of two almost complete skeletons in the walled-up staircase leading to the Rood Loft, in the north wall of the Church, at the time of the restoration in 1891. The probable solution seems that the Commissioners, who visited Breage 22nd April, 1549, to ascertain that the injunctions of Edward VI. were duly fulfilled, ordered the destruction of the windows, as containing figures of the Saints and emblems of idolatry. Possibly also stone tombs were destroyed and desecrated, partly in a spirit of iconoclasm, and partly from the spirit of plunder. We can imagine at this juncture some one more pious or superstitious than his fellows gathering the fragments of beautiful glass, and bones torn from their tombs within the Church, and placing them in the cavity of the broken stairway in process of being walled up.*

The granite support of the Credence Table and the Piscina in the chancel were exhumed from the foundations of the Church during the restoration and placed in their original situation ; also the rose Piscina and the pedestal on which it at present stands were unearthed at this time. The pedestal in question, it may be stated, has nothing whatever to do with the Piscina, the date of which is most probably coeval with the Church, but is evidently the base of a font of Jacobean origin. The granite bowl masquerading as a stoup in the porch is not of ecclesiastical origin at all ; its original use was evidently for grinding corn in primitive times. It may be interesting to mention the discovery during the restoration, beneath the floor of the Church, near where the pulpit now stands, of six skeletons lying uncoffined side by side, the skulls of all of them being perforated with bullet wounds ; the teeth in each skull were almost perfect, suggestive of violent and untimely deaths. The story of this tragedy has long since faded into oblivion ; possibly these skeletons belonged to victims of some fierce act of military discipline or retaliation in the Parliamentary Wars.

The restoration of Germoe Church was taken in hand a century earlier than that of Breage, for what reason it is impossible to say. At this period the mining operations of the Parish were mainly centred round Germoe, from Trewarvas Head to Laseve, and between the two hills of Tregoning and Godolphin. It may well have been that the restoration of Germoe Church was begun at an earlier date because it stood in the most populous portion of the parish. Sometime in the fourteenth century a north aisle was added to the small Norman cruciform Church, and then a little later a further enlargement and embellishment was made by the addition of

*It is possible that this vandalism may have been committed during the time of Independent ascendancy.

the north transept, and the present chancel to some extent reared upon Norman foundations ; the south transept, as we have previously stated, was of Norman origin. For some reason or other, the work seems to have been arrested when half carried through ; the builders had gone as far as to replace the Norman arch in the south transept by a twin archway,* the natural development of which would have been the addition of a south arcade. Instead of this the present south doorway was added to the Church, superseding an earlier entrance. The porch built over this door was not added until the next century, possibly about the time of the rebuilding of Breage Church. The grotesque carvings of monkeys on the corbel stones supporting the ends of the copings of the porch have evidently been taken from the older building. A feature of the chancel at Germoe is the canopied arch over the present sedilia and piscina. I take it that this beautiful arched aperture originally contained a tomb, possibly of a de Pengersick, or it may have been used as a sepulchre in connection with the Easter Festival ; at any-rate, its true significance has long been lost sight of under the hand of the spoiler and the restorer.

The most interesting feature for the ecclesiastical anti-quarian is not the Church itself, but the curious edifice in the Churchyard, known as St. Germoe's Chair. Tradition says this was erected by a member of the de Pengersick family. When Leland, the great antiquary, visited Cornwall in the reign of Henry VIII., he mentions both St. Germoe's Tomb, St. Germoe's Chair and St. Germoe's Well. The water still gurgles and bubbles from the spring by the roadside, from whence the Saint slaked his thirst and supplied his simple wants, but the very site of his tomb is long forgotten, the crude and vulgar bigotry of an intervening age having no place in its system for such memories. Germoe's Chair has been the fruitful source of many curious speculations and

*See Sedding's "Norman Architecture in Cornwall."

ingenious theories as to its origin. There can be but little doubt, however, that its original use was in connection with the Palm Sunday celebrations of the mediæval Church. It seems to have been customary on Palm Sundays for some of the Clergy, bearing a cross which was covered or muffled at some point in the service, to issue from the Church, followed by a portion of the congregation in procession bearing palms or their substitutes in their hands. A booth was erected in the Churchyard; sometimes this was of stone and of a permanent character like Germoe's Chair. Arrived at this erec-

St. Germoe's Chair.

tion the officiating Priest read the Gospel for the day; at this point another procession issued from the Church, headed by a Priest bearing the Host, and a number of children following a cross, decorated with wreaths of green leaves and singing "Blessed is He that cometh in the name of the Lord." The two groups then mingled together, the muffled cross was removed, and a distribution of bread or alms was made from the booth or pavilion, or, as in the case of Germoe, from what is now called Germoe's Chair. The united processions then, following the Priests, returned to the Church, where the service was continued to its close.*

Cornwall from its position escaped the turmoil of the Wars of the Roses. During this outwardly brutal and sordid period, whilst the Barons were hacking themselves in pieces, and successive Kings were merely "landlords" of England for the time being, the true heart of the nation was beginning to throb slowly with the pulses of a new life. I doubt much if Master William Pensans and his successors onward to Sir William Pers, and their flocks at Breage and Germoe, troubled themselves very much about the battles and rebellions and judicial murders that made up the history of England during the times in which they lived. Rumours of these terrible stirrings would be brought to them from time to time by wandering Friars or the Pilgrims passing through the Parish on their way to St. Michael's Mount, which was then one of the most popular places of pilgrimage in England. Doubtless many of the Pilgrims would make Breage the last halting place for the night, and move on to St. Michael's Mount on the following morning. These Pilgrims would be a motley crew of every class and grade, some seeking no doubt for the forgiveness of heinous deeds and crimes through the mediation of St. Michael, others seeking health and often finding it, not by the help of the Saint but through change of air and scene. Childless parents of great possessions often made pilgrimages to distant shrines in search of an heir, and still others were pilgrims because they loved change and to live close to Nature, though perhaps they never knew it.

In 1471 after the Battle of Barnet a strange band of Pilgrims visited St. Michael's Mount. John, Earl of Oxford, who had escaped from the slaughter of that terrible battle, came by sea to the Mount with a band of followers disguised

---

*See Walcott's "Sacred Archæology" pp. 421, 423. Also Dr. Roch's "Church of our Fathers," etc.

as Pilgrims.　They landed, simulating deep devotion, and obtaining admittance to the Castle, drew arms from beneath their Pilgrims' cloaks and rushed upon and overpowered the small garrison.　Sir John Arundell of Lanherne, who was sent to retake the Castle, was slain in the attempt on the sands between the Mount and the shore—in his death, it is said, fulfilling a curse of former years.　After a siege of six months the Earl of Oxford and his men surrendered upon terms, the Earl being allowed to retire to France, from whence he returned with Henry of Richmond, to share in the victory of Bosworth Field.

Pilgrims, wandering, preaching Friars and merchants, who came to the West for the purchase of tin, would practically at this time be the sole sources of news and connecting links with the outer world.　Men then led isolated lives, less dependent upon their fellows for daily needs and wants. The phrase "we are all members one of another" has a fuller and deeper meaning for us than it had for them.

We cannot conclude the account of this period without a brief allusion to the names of the incumbents from the time of David de Lyspein onwards.　The particulars of their lives have long since faded into oblivion ; whether good or bad, wise or foolish, their memories have utterly faded.　The fact of the nationality, however, of many of them survives in their names.　Henry Cretier (1362) from his name we take to have been one of the swarm of French Priests that at this time were spread over the country.　The great majority of the others seem to have been Cornishmen : Sir John Yurl bears a name common enough amongst the Cornish Clergy at this time.　Sir William Pellour of course was one of the numerous Cornish family of Pellar and Sir William Pers would now be known as William Pearce.　Sir John Gode or Ude bears also a name common in the Cornish Priesthood of the period. Sir William Lehe (1445) was, we fancy, from the Penwith Peninsula, from the similarity of his name to the name of a

E

manor in that district. Master William of Penzance (1403) and Master Thomas Godolphin (1505) were, of course, undoubtedly Cornishmen, the latter, we are led to conclude, being a son of Sir John Godolphin, Sheriff of Cornwall in 1504, the founder of the fortunes of his family. Of the lives of these men, alas! we can know nothing, beyond the fact that in varying degrees they testified to the unseen and spiritual, and, in spite of imperfections and weaknesses, held up the torch of a Divine light for the illumination of a dark and degraded age.

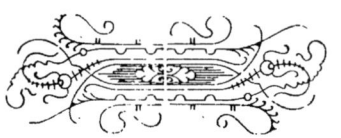

The Reformation to the end of the Commonwealth.

CHAPTER IV.

Master John Jakes, bachelor in decrees, of whom we know nothing beyond the fact that he died and was buried in Breage churchyard, became Vicar in 1510, when no cloud loomed upon the ecclesiastical horizon. He who at that date had foretold the ultimate consequences of the marriage of Henry VIII. to a Spanish Princess would have been put down as a fool and a dreamer. It would have seemed obvious to the ecclesiastical politicians of that day that if the marriage affected at all the fortunes of the Church it would be in the direction of drawing closer the bonds with Rome. Possibly, here and there, there may have been those who saw the signs of the coming of the storm in what seemed to them a more or less distant future ; and probably they dismissed the uncomfortable thought with the sixteenth century equivalent of "*après moi le déluge.*" Yet within thirty years the deluge had been unloosed and swept all before it. Within three years of the demise of John Jakes the great Abbey of Hayles, with its broad acres and vast patronage, was dissolved ; its stately buildings and magnificent Church were falling into ruins, turned into stone quarries for new mansions, and its Brethren scattered, never to be re-united.

John Jakes was succeeded in 1536 by John Bery, M.A., the last Vicar to be appointed by the Abbot and Convent of Hayles. Breage escaped the terrible ecclesiastical tempest that in places less remote was sweeping all before it. Though Hayles Abbey was in ruins and the Brethren scattered, things continued in this little far-away appanage of the great House much in the same way as heretofore, until the terrible year

1549. The Cornish, like the people of Wales, were bitterly opposed to the Reformation in all its works and ways, and would have none of it. As an instance of West Country methods in dealing with the new innovations, we may quote the case of the parishioners of Sampford Courtenay, on the northern skirts of the great waste of Dartmoor. On Sunday, 9th June, 1549, the new service in English was used for the first time in place of the Mass, in compliance with the royal injunctions. The people would have none of it, and on the following day compelled the Parish Priest, under threats of what they would do to him, to resume his vestments and say Mass as usual. In the April of this same year the storm had broken in all its violence in our own part of Cornwall. Commissioners had been sent throughout the County to examine the Churches and have all images found in them removed and destroyed, and also, in plain language, to plunder the Churches of their valuable plate, jewels and vestments, in the specious name of religion. The Commissioners were required to inquire into the doctrinal character of the preaching in the various Churches, and to ascertain that the services were no longer held in Latin but in the English tongue. A Commissioner named Body was making his official examination at Helston Church—bent, no doubt, like the majority of his fellows, on spoil as well as iconoclasm—when he was stabbed to death by an enraged Priest, who had attended the visitation in the company of one Kiltor of St. Keverne. This spark set the county, already smouldering with discontent, in a blaze of rebellion. The people, under the influence of the Clergy, flocked together from various parts of the County, committing many barbarous outrages. Humphrey Arundell of St. Michael's Mount placed himself at the head of this rapidly-growing rabble of peasantry, and with many of the Clergy the march upon Exeter was begun.

Job Militon of Pengersick Castle was at the time Sheriff of the County, but he was powerless in the face of a force that by the time Bodmin was reached had grown to six thousand strong. It is curious to note that this enthusiastic but undisciplined host, marching to its doom, under the walls of Exeter, contained within itself a strong leaven of socialism. It seems to have been generally agreed, at any rate amongst the rank and file, that all land should in future be held in common, and that all enclosing fences should be obliterated. A few years previously Germany had been throbbing with the same spirit, and the German Peasants had been moved to throw off the yoke of the oppressing nobles, their minds full of dreams of a sixteenth century millennium. Both these efforts, due to opposite trains of events, had their origin in the spirit of the age striving vaguely after dim ideals, and both were trampled on and extinguished with ruthless force and cruelty. Humphrey Arundell perished on the scaffold, and thousands of his deluded followers in the fields and bye-ways, cut down by a merciless soldiery.

John Bery seems to have preferred monotony and safety at Breage to a life of adventure in the field; at any rate, he lived on as Vicar of Breage till the day of his death in 1558. He doubtlessly conformed outwardly, if not in his heart, to the new order of things, and in the reign of Queen Mary conformed back again to the old order. Death absolved him in 1558 from a further change of opinions on the accession of Elizabeth in that year.

The terrible memories of 1549 would long linger in the minds of John Bery and the people of Breage. Some, no doubt, from Breage, had joined the ill-fated march to Exeter to return no more.

The reports of the Commissioners who visited Germoe on the 18th April, and Breage on the 22nd April, 1549, are as follows : " Germoe, Minister, Henry Nicol, a Cope of blue damask, one set of very coarse vestments, a copper gilt cross, two chalices, one gilt the other parcel-gilt, two small bells, a fair brass censer, a linen streamer with a cross upon it of red silk.' The inventory closes with the remark that nothing has been sold for a year past.[*]

The list at Breage reveals vessels and vestments of a richer and more valuable character. The list comprises three chalices of silver, of which two were gilt, three linen towels upon the altar, one pair of vestments of blue velvet, one purple, broidered with gold work, a pair of vestments of white satin, a pair of tawny satin, another pair of oldsay, a cope of Morys velvet, purple broidered in gold work, an old cope of blue velvet, two candlesticks of latten on the altar, upon the font a yard of linen cloth, an old rotten streamer of silk, and four bells of large burden hanging in the tower. Such was the inventory of spoils in this remote parish at the time of the Great Pillage.

The Church must have had a deep hold on the hearts of the Cornish people at the time of the Reformation, or they would never have risen in her defence in the way they did in 1549. The mutilation and desecration of her shrines stirred the hearts of the people to the very depths. The same spirit of devotion to the Church was manifest also in a marked degree in Wales; indeed, until the Reformation the Welsh were of all the inhabitants of the British Isles the most devoted to the cause of the Church: where she was once strongest she is now weakest. In pre-Reformation times the Feasts and Festivals of the Church in Cornwall were bound up with the social life of the people, and its ritual, paradoxical through it may seem in the present age, satisfied the deep emotional cravings of the Cornish character, whilst its teaching was in unison with the needs of their hearts. As an instance of the deep hold of the Church upon the pre-Reformation life of the people, we have in Breage the curious anomaly that the chief fête day of our Nonconformists is St. Stephen's Day, which is the Feast of the Dedication of the

---

[*]Kalendar of State Papers. Domestic Series.

Parish Church, whilst at Germoe the Festival of the patron Saint is kept by them as a day of teas and rejoicing.

Under the new order of things brought in by the Reformation there was no room for the play of emotions, the services of the Church were cold and bare, adapted for religious philosophers, but not for peasants; the change came, too, in the guise of an exotic planted by men of high station, whom the people regarded as their natural oppressors and the destroyers of the Church of their fathers. What followed was that which might have been expected—a gradual lapsing of the people into what was, to all intents and purposes, a crude form of paganism, which lasted, with the exception of some stirrings of the dry bones during the Commonwealth, until the coming of John Wesley, who with the warm glow of emotional fervour re-converted the Cornish peasantry in the main to Christianity. If proof of this assertion were needed, it is only necessary to compare the religious aspect of things in Cornwall and Brittany at the present day. Both people belong to the same division of the Celtic race, yet both now in the main stand at opposite poles in politics and religion. The reason seems to lie in the fact that the Cornish were deprived of a faith which they loved, and which satisfied the emotional and materialistic cravings of their hearts, and that the new Clergy, creatures and toadies of the great, utterly failed to appeal to their sympathies and to win their affections.

In 1558 Sir Alexander Dawe, the last of the "Sirs," became Vicar of Breage, and continued as such until the day of his death in 1595. The record of his burial is still extant in the Parish Registers. He was presented to the living of Breage by one Richard Hyde, who had become, by purchase, patron of the Benefice for one turn only. The Abbot and Convent of Hayles had followed the policy of the other religious houses at the dissolution of the Monasteries, and saved what property they could from the impending catastrophe by granting, where possible, long leases of the Abbey lands and selling the next presentations to their ecclesiastical patronage.

A dark and terrible shadow passed over the life of the parish during the time of Alexander Dawe. Breage was visited in 1578 by a pestilence, which we have little doubt was the terrible Black Death or Plague, which at this time was claiming endless victims all over the land. We who live in these days of practical security from such awful visitations can have no idea of the horror and dismay which they inspired, and the misery and desolation which they spread broadcast over the land. To realise the horror of the Plague, let us imagine an epidemic as contagious and as infectious as influenza was some few years ago spreading everywhere, the great majority of its victims dying in the most terrible sufferings. The epidemic of plague in question had first appeared in London in the autumn of 1563 ; about a thousand persons dying each week during the latter part of 1563 and the earlier part of 1564. In 1570 Newcastle and in 1574 Edinburgh endured terrible visitations of this scourge. During the last months of 1578 and the earlier months of 1579 the Breage burial register contains the record of seventy-six burials in Breage churchyard. No comment is made upon the nature of the disease, but there can be but little doubt we have here the grim records of a visit of the terrible Black Death, whose dark shadow at this time hung in awful menace over the whole land. The words of the Litany, "from plague, pestilence and famine, from battle and murder and from sudden death, good Lord deliver us," had a fulness of meaning for our fathers which we who live in a brighter, cleaner and more peaceful time can only dimly realise.

With the death of Sir Alexander Dawe, the last link with the old pre-Reformation life was severed ; henceforward the stream of parochial life was to run in channels more closely approximating to those of our own age, and succeeding

Vicars were men of different antecedents and ways. The patronage of the Living, though nominally in the hands of the Crown, came practically to be in the gift of the Godolphin family, which had risen to a position of power and influence in the preceding hundred years.

Francis Harvey, who succeeded Alexander Dawe, was the son of Sir Anthony Harvey, Kt., and Lucy Lister of Swarland, near Felton, in Northumberland. The family of Harvey was remotely connected with the Godolphin family, through the Carews.* Francis Harvey was born 2nd March, 1562. He was educated at Corpus Christi College, Cambridge, but migrated, after taking his B.A. degree, to Emmanuel College, which had been recently founded by his relative, William Mildmay, as the home of a mild and aristocratic form of Puritanism. It is interesting to note that Sir William Godolphin, who died in 1613, was at Emmanuel College at the same time as Francis Harvey. Perhaps it may not be too fanciful to conclude that an intimacy between William Godolphin and Francis Harvey ripened into close friendship in the quiet Cambridge home of Puritan learning, and that thus the son of a Northumberland squire came to settle in the remote West. Francis Harvey married Mary Yorke, a lady of ancient family, in Phillack Church, in 1595; their descendants were long settled at Maen in this County.

Soon after obtaining the living of Breage, Francis Harvey was preferred to the living of St. Erth, which he continued to hold jointly with Breage until the day of his death. Whilst the Reformation had struck at many evils, it had left one of the greatest of the abuses of the Church practically untouched. One of the chief factors in preparing the popular mind for the Reformation was the abuse of Church patronage; French and Italian Priests, in many cases not speaking the English language, had been foisted upon the English people,

---

* MS. in the possession of Fleet-Surgeon Harvey.

to the exclusion of their own kith and kin. This evil system had begun with the Conquest and had continued right down to the Reformation, accentuated and intensified by the fact that a single person was capable of holding numerous benefices, which in many cases he had never seen, to the exclusion of others worthier and holier than himself. It was this condition of things that alone rendered the Reformation possible. The storm of the Reformation burst, but swept in vain round this crowning abuse. After the Reformation the abuse of patronage presented itself even in more odious forms, and the best life of the Church withered and died under its poisonous shadow. Francis Harvey was not an excessive pluralist; he held only two livings, though his cousin, William Cotton, who succeeded him, enjoyed a good baker's dozen or more.

An event happened in the first few months of the incumbency of Francis Harvey which would long linger in the minds of his flock, and which for years to come would be spoken of by the cottage and farm house evening firesides. The 23rd July, 1595 was a hot summer's day; a thick haze lay over the sea, which gradually lifted, disclosing four Spanish ships of war lying off the coast, over against Mousehole. Their hostile intentions were soon evident; boatloads of armed men began to put off from the ships. A force of over two hundred Spaniards was quickly landed without opposition. The little town of Mousehole was soon in flames, and a handful of brave men who scorned flight perished at their own doors.[*]

The Spanish force streamed up the hill[†] their course marked by blazing roof-trees. The old grey village Church of Paul on the ridge soon became the special object of their fury, and its stones to this day bear grim witness to the devouring flames that once enveloped them. The inhabitants of Mousehole fled in a terrified mob towards Penzance, the roar of

[*]Paul Church Burial Registers.
[†]Carew's Survey of Cornwall.

the ships' guns adding speed to their flight. It seems Sir Francis Godolphin had ridden forth earlier in the day from Godolphin House, and saw either from Godolphin or Tregoning Hill the dense clouds of smoke hanging over Mousehole and Paul, whilst the booming of the guns of the four warships in the Bay would speedily make the whole situation clear to the mind of this keen soldier trained in the Irish Wars under Essex. Without delay he spurred his horse to the scene of action and encountered the flying crowd a little westward of Penzance. He succeeded for a time in infusing something of his own brave spirit into the minds of the fugitives and the men of Penzance capable of bearing arms. A move was made upon the Spanish position, and the Spaniards, seeing the advancing force, retired to their ships, only again after a short period to disembark at Newlyn, which they speedily set on fire, and began to move on Penzance. In vain, sword in hand, the brave Sir Francis endeavoured to rally the people to the defence of their town and homes; he was speedily deserted by all save a few of his own servants. As the Spaniards entered the town he had no alternative but to ride away, surrounded by his little company of brave followers.

The Spaniards remained in Penzance Bay until the 25th July, when they put out to sea in a north-west breeze, just in time to escape capture by a force of British ships rounding the Lizard, which they must have seen in the offing. The anxiety and dread of the people of Breage, standing with straining eyes watching the course of events in the plain below during those two fateful days, must have been great indeed. One wild rumour after another of dire deeds transpiring beneath them, by the sea, would pass through their midst. There would be little sleep in the village during the two anxious nights the Spanish warships lay in Penzance Bay. Many minds would turn to another night of anxiety and dread a few years before, when the great Armada had passed the Lizard early in the forenoon, and was making its way up Channel, followed by the English Fleet.

> " For swift to East and swift to West the ghastly war flame
>> spread,
>> High on St. Michael's Mount it shone ; it shone on Beachy
>> Head."

Francis Harvey died whilst still practically a young man, 2nd March, 1607. We copy from our burial register the almost pathetic entry recording his death and burial, so different is it by contrast to the endless laconic entries of death that precede and follow it. Evidently the entry was made by the hand of one who knew and loved him. It is written in a clear and elegant hand, and the entry carries with it something of truthfulness and sincerity that brings the image of Francis Harvey up out of the mists of the past, as that of a true and good man of a mild and gentle type of Puritan piety. The entry is as follows :—"*Francisus Harvey, theologus hujusque parochiæ Vicarius cum jam quadragesimum quartum annum ætatis vix attigesset. Secundo die Marcii extremum diem clausit, et ut per totum temporis curriculum transegit vitam minime non inhonestam sic obiit, mortem non minus plane piam. Sepultusque fuit die quarto tunc proximum insequente. Anno Domini 1607.*"

Francis Harvey was succeeded by his cousin, William Cotton, M.A., described in the Exeter Registers as "the beloved son of the Bishop." He resigned the living of Breage after holding it but little over a year. Walker, in his "Sufferings of the Clergy," includes William Cotton in his list of suffering Clergy during the Commonwealth. However deeply the sufferings of William Cotton may have touched the feelings of a former age, they are not likely to move the sympathies of our own. As well as being Vicar of Breage, he was also Precentor and a residentiary Canon of Exeter Cathedral, and held the livings of Silverton, Whimple and Duloe, and possibly others at one and the same time. His brother, Edward Cotton, was equally well provided for by his father. It was outrageous pluralism of this kind that alienated the people from the Church and prepared the way for the wild outpourings of religious bigotry and frenzy under the Commonwealth. William Cotton, with the failure of the royal cause, was compelled to resign the mass of patronage which he held. He died at his seat of Bottreux Castle in 1649 or 1650. Walker informs us that in his veins " flowed the blood of crowned heads of England, Scotland and Ireland, and other great personages of the highest rank," and that " he was a person of a meek and humble spirit, of a grave and sober conversation, of exemplary piety, charity and learning."

Edward Cotton was succeeded by William Orchard in 1608. In the record of his institution in the Episcopal Registers he is described as " Preacher of the Word of God " ; this phrase will perhaps serve to disclose the bias of his mind and the theological bent of the times. Unlike his predecessors Harvey and Cotton, he had graduated at no University. Most possibly in his own mind he regarded such institutions as unnecessary for one who was led by the Spirit of God. It is possible that he owed his appointment to the living of Breage to Sir William Godolphin, the then Squire of Godolphin, and friend of the statesman Cecil, who, it seems more than probable, acquired a Puritan bias when a student at Emmanuel College, the Cambridge home of Puritanism.

I rather conclude from the frequent mention of the name of Orchard in the Breage Registers about the time of his incumbency, that his family had been settled in the parish at the time of his appointment. A George Orchard married a Dorcas Coode of Methleigh, and an Edward Orchard married a Jane Sparnon of Sparnon. The Coodes and Sparnons at this time, with the exception of the Godolphins, were the chief families of the parish, ranking considerably above the rank of yeoman. William Orchard became a widower in 1619. The record in the Breage Register of the death and burial of his wife is as follows: "*Anna Orchard uxor Wilhelmi Orchard, Vicarii hujus parochiæ, filia Johis Yeo, gent, died 9th Feb. and was buried 11th Feb. 1619.*" His daughter Mary married John Coode of Methleigh; their descendant owns the estate of Methleigh at the present time.

Whilst Sir William Godolphin and Parson Orchard were both Puritans, they were both loyalists. They would have shuddered with horror "at those days which were coming upon the earth," and which to a great extent were the logical outcome of the Puritanism which they and others professed acting upon the popular mind; they were putting new wine into old bottles, regardless of the inevitable result, as good men will do in every age. Though Sir William Godolphin was not destined to see the day that his king perished on the scaffold, it was the lot of William Orchard to see it forty years later, and ultimately for conscience sake to be ejected from his home and office. Rather than be untrue to the light within him, like so many of his brethren, William Orchard elected to go into the wilderness. It was his lot never to return to his benefice, though his son at the Restoration petitioned Parliament on his behalf for revenues from the living of Breage, of which he deemed his father to have been defrauded.

It was during William Orchard's incumbency that Breage for the first and last time was favoured with a royal visit in the person of Charles, Prince of Wales, afterwards Charles II. When the royal cause was irretrievably lost, Charles fled to Cornwall on his way to seek refuge in the Scilly Islands. For some days he rested at Godolphin House, and what remains of the suite of rooms he occupied is still shewn there. It would be interesting to know how Charles spent the few days of his sojourn in Breage, and how he wiled the time away, and whether, after the good custom of those days, in spite of the danger of his position, he joined in the

Sunday worship at Breage Church. It is possible to picture the swarthy youthful face, with the thick heavy red lips and with *ennui* written upon it, looking wearily from the Godolphin aisle upon William Orchard, as hand upon hour-glass he unfolded Puritan truth from a maze of conflicting facts.

But the evil days drew on apace; Prince and Parson had alike to go before the storm. Soon after the swearing of the Solemn League and Covenant by Parliament in 1644, the tithes of Breage were sequestrated or confiscated by the Government; *William Orchard with Antony Randall, curate of Germoe, and Robert Smith, curate of Cury, were thus reduced to dire poverty. Their parishioners, touched by their trials, and regarding them no doubt as honest and faithful men, on the 8th May, 1649, petitioned Parliament that a yearly grant might be made to them of £40 each out of the confiscated tithes of St. Keverne. Their prayer was answered, but after four years of weary waiting, the tried clerics complained to Parliament that their grants had been withheld by the County Committee, and humbly requested "that the rents may remain in the Tenants' hands." On the 17th August, 1653, the County Committee made answer to Parliament, that " by information of Colonel Rous, M.P., the Vicarage of Breage is sufficiently endowed, and that the Ministers thereof are malignant and scandalous, and that Antony Rous of Wotton, John Bawden of Trelask, and three others are appointed trustees for disposing of the grant made by Parliament to four such able and godly ministers as they shall judge meet to place in their room." Whilst the hypocritical cant of this declaration provokes a smile, at the same time it arouses mournful reflections on the violence and bigotry that is ever wont to dog the steps of human effort after political and religious reformation.

" The able and godly minister " chosen to supplant

---

*Reports of the Committee of Compounding.

William Orchard at Breage was one James Innes. Doubtless
he was a man of extreme opinions both in politics and religion,
but like William Orchard in the hour of darkness he was able
to play the true man, and rather than conform at the Restoration to tenets in which he did not believe, he vacated
his office even before Black Bartholomew's Day, 24th August,
1662. He found an asylum in Scotland in the household of
the Earl of Lauderdale, where he performed the office of
chaplain in conformity with the Presbyterian use.

The seeds of Puritanism sown by men like Orchard and
Innes did not die, but lay germinating in the hearts of the
Cornish people, rendering possible the great work of John
Wesley a hundred years later. Such men succeeded in a great
measure in destroying the pre-Reformation mechanical ideals
of salvation in the hearts of the people, which prepared the
way for the stirring of the dry bones in future years.

Richard Carew's Survey of Cornwall, published in 1602,
gives a vivid picture of the conditions of life in Cornwall
prevailing during the period we have been considering in
this chapter. The condition of the mining population, he
tells us, was much worse than that of the agricultural population.* We gather from his pages that the wages of the
miners were so inadequate that sooner or later indigence
compelled them to have recourse to their employers, who
supplied them with food and clothing in advance of their
wages at usurious prices. The Stannary Courts, we are informed, were utterly corrupt and saturated with the spirit of
perjury and injustice.* The houses of the working people,
we gather at this period, were made of clay, possessing
neither windows nor any attempt at ceiling or plastering* ; a
hole in the wall being considered sufficient to do duty for a
chimney. The miner and labouring people generally, we
gather, were alike destitute of shoes and stockings, and we
may add, of course, of any rudiments of education.

*Carew's Survey of Cornwall pp. 49, 59, 183, etc.

Leland, when he visited the parish, found large mining works along the coast from Trewarvas Head to Praa Sands. Sir Francis Godolphin a generation later developed the ancient mines of Great Work and Wheal Vor upon scientific principles and a scale of vastness hitherto undreamt of.

The mines, it is evident, brought riches and prosperity to the owners of the soil, but not to the people who dwelt upon it; to them, as Carew makes clear, they meant too often degradation and oppression. The harvest of this evil sowing is still being reaped at the present day. It is but too true that with the Reformation the people lost a powerful protector in the Church. With all her faults—and they were many- until the Reformation the Church had been consistently the friend of the poor ; her clergy until that period, had been the members of a great corporation, and as such stood in no dread of "the petty tyrant of the fields." With the coming of the Reformation all was changed, and the Parish Priest became too often the creature and parasite of the wealthy, moved but too frequently by fear and policy to neglect the claims of his flock, with for three centuries, disastrous results alike for Church and people. The people at the Reformation were ready to rise and to die for the Church, as we have seen in our own neighbourhood ; three centuries later they regarded her with utter suspicion and disfavour. Few with any acquaintance with the facts of the case will deny that the material and moral condition of the people, under much cruel injustice and exploitation, grew worse for some generations after the Reformation, because there were none to hold the balance of justice between class and class and stay the hand of the oppressor, at any rate in the remote places of the country.

In the western part of the County the mines tended to produce an utter neglect of agriculture, the effects of which were bad in every way. They also led to the reckless destruction of

F

much valuable timber for the purpose of making mine props. Western Cornwall, now so denuded and bare of trees, in ancient days was thickly wooded ; round Ashton now not a tree is to be seen, yet the name perpetuates the memory of the time when Ashton was the Down where the ash trees grew.

Carew tells us that there were few sheep in Cornwall in his days, and that those there were had little bodies and fleeces so coarse that their wool went by the name of Cornish hair. The horses, he says, were small and hardy and "quick travellers over rough and hilly country," but he goes on to say that by hard treatment and overwork they were soon worn out and rendered unfit for service. Owing to the practical absence of roads till long after Carew's time, vehicular traffic was practically impossible ; horses were therefore used as pack animals, and a regular system of transit of goods prevailed through the County by means of pack horses. The tracks that passed by the name of roads* for the six rainy months of the year, were practically impassable quagmires of mud, making intercourse, save of the most urgent character, practically impossible. It was on account of the extreme difficulty of communication through the long winter months that the gentry of the district established for themselves town houses in Helston, in which they might exchange the isolation of the country for some measure of friendly and agreeable intercourse.

The land used for tillage seems to have been chiefly manured with sea sand and sea weed ; the little ploughing there was would, of course, be done by oxen, a method which at any rate had the merit of producing a strong and vigorous breed of cattle, which in size would perhaps more than favourably compare with some of the animals to be seen at the present time.

---

*Carew says "There are not any roads in the whole kingdom worse than ours, hastily repaired only when some great man passes that way in his coach."

We gather from Carew "that some gentlemen allowed their cattle to go wild in their woods and waste ground, where they were hunted and killed with crossbows and pieces after the manner of deer." At this time the Deer Park attached to Godolphin House took in a large part of the present parish of Godolphin; the remains of the high walls of this ancient park may still be seen on the south-western slopes of Godolphin Hill.

In Carew's time the women and children of the West of Cornwall carried on the industry of mat-making to a large extent. These mats were made of coarse grass, and were exported to London in great numbers for the purpose of floor and wall coverings.

Carew informs us that the Cornish had no oaths and never swore, but that they made up for it by a plentiful indulgence in curses, maledictions and the giving of spiteful nicknames.

The two chief practising physicians[*] in the County in Carew's time were Rawe Clyes, a blacksmith, and a Mr. Atwell, parson of St. Tue; the latter obtained the most wonderful results from recommending a diet of apples and milk.

The chief pastimes of the country people at this period, as far as can be ascertained, were wrestling, hurling and shooting with arrows. The game of hurling, in both its forms, seems to have been even more rough and dangerous than Cornish wrestling, and was attended, if Carew speak correctly, frequently with fatal results and serious injury to life and limb; yet he goes on to say " was never Attorney or Coroner troubled for the matter." It was in the larger game of "Hurling the County" that most of the serious damage was done; this wild game was played over miles of country by men both on horseback and on foot. The goals were as a rule a couple of towns or villages three or four miles apart. The match seems to have been arranged, in the first place, between two country gentlemen, who on the occasion

---

[*]Carew p. 172.

of some appointed holiday would gather as their respective supporters, as far as possible, the male inhabitants of two or three neighbouring parishes. Each squire headed the mob he had thus raised to the appointed rendezvous. When the two masses of men, under their respective commanders, were brought face to face, at an appointed signal, a silver ball was thrown into the air. The object of the game was for each side to endeavour to capture the ball and carry it to their own goal some miles distant, in spite of the efforts of their opponents to hinder them in their purpose. The struggle would be waged over miles of country, to the right side or to the left, through rivers, ditches, woods and bogs, the ball being now passed from one on foot to one on horseback, no effort being spared to drag the possessor of the ball to the earth by the opposing side. Little wonder that such a game often resulted in deaths and serious maimings.

A Cornish amusement of a milder character that came to an end with the seventeenth century was the performance of the ancient Miracle Plays. A vestige of the custom still survives in some places in the bands of children who at Christmas time go from house to house, dressed to impersonate a medley of characters, repeating garbled snatches of doggerel, which are in reality fragments of the ancient plays in the last stage of evolution and disintegration. In their earliest form the Miracle Plays were performed by the Clergy in their Churches to illustrate to an ignorant age, alike without literature and the faculty of using it, the truths of the Christian religion. These plays continued to be performed in Churches to a greater or less extent down to the time of the Reformation.† The Reformation endeavoured to draw an unreal line of demarcation between sacred and profane, and the drama thus came to be placed beyond the pale as worthless and sinful, with the natural disastrous result that it became quickly degraded

†See the Article "Drama" in "Encylopædia Britannica" by Mr. A. W. Ward.

and debased, like many other harmless, healthful and pleasure-giving institutions and pastimes.

The Miracle Plays that have come down to us in the Cornish language[*] are first the Ordinalia : this is a trilogy consisting of the Plays of the Beginning of the World, the Passion and the Resurrection, with an interlude on the death of Pilate; this work is based on a French original of the fourteenth century. Secondly, we have the Play of the Life of St. Meriasek, of Breton parentage ; and lastly, a work based on the Ordinalia, containing many more English words, written by William Jordan, of Helston, in 1611; the work deals with the Creation of the World and the Deluge. The Cornish language was spoken in the West of Cornwall until the beginning of the eighteenth century[†] ; by the close of that century it had entirely disappeared. In Carew's time the Cornish Miracle Plays were performed in the open fields, and were resorted to by the country people with great delight; he tells us however, by his time they had become vulgarized and depraved to no small extent, possibly by the introduction of bucolic gag of a Rabelaisian character.

Judging from the pages of Carew, in the seventeenth century, with all its grossness and barbarism, there was much real friendship and happy intercourse amongst the people, possibly more than there is now. The Harvest Homes, the Church Ales and the Church Festivals of Dedication, with the Guary or Miracle Plays, all led to much friendly intercourse and hospitality. Carew says on these occasions, " the neighbour parishes lovingly visit one another " ; friends came from a distance, and were hospitably entertained with resultant kindliness and good fellowship. The Church Ales seem to have been run on much the same lines as the present Harvest Teas, with the exception that instead of tea, beer and cider were drunk, and that the venue of the

---

[*]See the Article in " Encyclopædia Britannica " by Mr. W. K Sullivan.
[†]Dr. Edward Lhuyd, "Archæologia Britannica" 1707, quoted by Mr. Jenner in his "Handbook of the Cornish Language."

feasting was laid at the Public House, instead of the village School or Institute.

Perhaps we shall obtain the most accurate glimpse of the character of the people, and the state of Western Cornwall generally at this period, from the State Papers. Here are a few gleanings culled at random from this source. In 1526 a Portuguese ship was wrecked at Gunwalloe and much cargo saved. It was seized by the servants of John Militon, of Pengersick, Thomas St. Aubyn and William Godolphin, and when the owner appealed to the Justices he was told it was the custom of the country, and that no redress was possible. A commission of enquiry ensued, followed by Star Chamber proceedings, and the defence was the usual one, for which any number of witnesses could always be obtained, that the owner had sold his property on the sea shore !

In 1575 an information of fifteen Articles was laid against Sir William Godolphin and the Killigrews, of Arwenack ; thirteen of these concerned piracy.

In 1582 a Spanish ship put into Falmouth ; she was boarded by a gang of men, who after removing the cargo as booty to Arwenack, took the ship to Ireland, throwing the crew overboard on the voyage. A Cornish Jury afterwards found there was no evidence to show by whom the deed was done. The Privy Council came to the conclusion very quickly that the plot originated with and was carried out by the orders of Lady Killigrew, of Arwenack.

In 1603 a Marseilles ship was plundered and the cargo carried to the Scilly Islands. The owner appealed to Sir Francis Godolphin, who made an order to his son John, then Governor of those Islands, to restore the cargo. John Godolphin expelled the unfortunate owner from the Islands and he could obtain no further redress.

In 1626 a Flemish privateer, which had been hovering like a bird of prey around the South-Western coast, was driven ashore and wrecked. The country people must have enjoyed the wrecking of this hostile ship with even more than their usual zest.

Dr. Borlase, writing in 1795, describes the methods of the mining population near the coast in his day in dealing with vessels in distress. His description would no doubt do equally well for the period we are considering. He says " The wreckers were mostly Tinners, who as soon as a ship was seen sailing near the coast left their work and equipped themselves with axes, and followed the ship along the coast, often to the number of two thousand men. They would cut a large trading vessel to pieces in one tide. They strip half-dead men of their clothing and cut down all who resist them."*

The following is a pleasing picture of the people of Germoe taken from a letter of the year 1710. " The people of Germoe, called Tinners, are a mad people, without fear of God or of the world. I cannot say a good word for them." Here is another extract from a letter of the period bearing date 30th October, 1671. " The Speedwell was cast away on the rocks at Pengersick. The rude people plundered her of all that was between decks, but the matter being noised about Sir William Godolphin, Mr. Hugh Boscawen and Mr. John St. Aubyn came to the wreck, and by their care preserved most of the goods from the violence of the country people."

It may well have been said of the Miners of Cornwall, as far as wrecking was concerned, " Wheresoever the carcase is, there will the vultures be gathered together." Mr. Hunt, in his " Popular Romances of the West of England," narrates a story of the mid-eighteenth century, which still lingers in the popular mind, of a terrible fight that took place between Miners from Breage and Wendron,

* From the Gwavas MS. in the British Museum. A letter from John Boson, of Newlyn, a Cornish-speaking Cornishman, written in the Cornish language. A copy of this letter was given to the Author by Henry Jenner, Esq.

over the spoils of a ship cast upon the rocks near the Lizard. In old times, it seems, a gigantic ash tree used to stand upon the Downs near Cury ; from its great size and the loneliness of its situation, it had in the course of time come to be a popular landmark. In the case of the wreck in question, the Wendron Tinners had the advantage over their Breage brethren in the matter of distance, and thus were able more quickly to fall upon the spoil, break up the unfortunate ship, and rifle the unhappy castaways of their belongings. Like the true artists they were in the art of appropriating the property of others, they worked quickly, and ere much time had elapsed they had reached the great ash tree of Cury on their journey home laden with spoil. Under this historic tree they encountered the band of Tinners from Breage, who soon realised from the rich booty in the hands of the men of Wendron that nothing more was to be done that day in the way of wrecking on the Lizard rocks. Baffled of their prey, and frantic with fury, the horde of men and women from Breage rushed upon their Wendron compatriots, and the tide of brutal fight raged for hours round the Cury ash tree. Mr. Hunt tells us that a Wendron man named Gluyas having been disabled was borne out of the fight by his friends, and placed upon the top of a hedge. A Breage woman named Prudy, seeing this paladin lying disabled on the hedge, rushed upon him exclaiming, " Ef thee art'nt ded, I'll make thee," and smote him upon the head with the iron upon her paton till he expired. Mr. Hunt concludes this story by stating that the fiend Prudy, as far as judicial investigation was concerned, was allowed to go untouched, because fights at this period between parishes were matters of such common occurrence as to excite but little comment, and fatal casualties so frequent as to be regarded as matters of no moment. In this statement, as we have seen, he is borne out by Carew writing in a previous generation. Down to fifty years ago the brutal system of

Parochial rivalry and violence continued, at any rate in a mitigated form. A friend wrote to Mr. Hunt : " So late as thirty years ago (circa 1850) it was unsafe to venture alone through the streets of the lower part of Helston after night-fall on a market day owing to the frays of the Breage, Wendron and Sithney men." This statement was fully borne out by an aged friend of the writer, now dead, who told him that in his youth even funeral processions of Miners brought to Breage from other parishes were assailed with showers of stones, and an attack which either ended in hasty retreat or a prolonged free fight. It may be added, however, that Sunday was kept as a truce of God, and on that day a dead Miner from outside the parish might be borne to his rest without an assault being delivered on his friends as they followed him to the grave. This aged friend also informed the writer that to such an extent did this brutal system of savagery prevail that no Miner could pass from his own parish to another without being assailed and maltreated. Indeed, whenever Miners crossed the borders of their own parishes, they did so in bodies for mutual protection. Well on into the first half of the last century, fighting seems to have been one of the chief topics of interest, if not the chief amusement of the neighbourhood, and fights for wagers were of constant occurrence in Breage parish, on Trew Green and elsewhere. To conclude this brief summary of past conditions, one cannot help feeling that there was something to be said for the old Roman view as to the results of the occupation of mining on human character. It is a dismal picture, truly, this of past conditions in the West of Cornwall, but when we contrast it with the present it fills the mind with hopefulness, and reveals the vast latent possibilities in human nature for improvement and progress. If out of this dark and barbarous past we have so recently emerged, what bright possibilities may not lie in the coming time seems but a reasonable thought.

RECENT TIMES.

CHAPTER V.

On the accession of Charles II. the intruding Puritan divine James Innes was quickly ejected. He found refuge for the remainder of his life in the household of the Earl of Lauderdale. It would seem that at the time of the ejection of Innes, William Orcharde had become too old and infirm to resume his office as vicar of Breage, and thus it came about that James Trewinnard, a member of the ancient family long settled at Trewinnard, in the Parish of St. Erth, succeeded to the benefice in 1661. He also held the living of Mawgan conjointly with that of Breage, according to the lax custom of the times. On his death, which took place at Mawgan, the parish in which he had chosen to reside, he was succeeded at Breage by Henry Huthnance. Judging by his name Henry Huthnance was of local origin, and at any rate was a connection of the family of Robinson, of Nansloe; he lies buried in Breage churchyard at the east end of the Chancel wall, between his predecessor, the learned and saintly Francis Harvey, and one of his successors, William Eusticke, of whom more anon. On the death of Henry Huthnance, in 1720, James Trewinnard, son of the former incumbent of that name, became vicar; like his father, he held jointly the two benefices of Breage and Mawgan. He was a graduate of Pembroke College, Cambridge. He was succeeded in 1722 by Edward Collins, bachelor of laws. This incumbent, like several of his predecessors, was also dowered with the living of St. Erth. Edward Collins was the son of the Reverend John Collins, vicar of Redruth, and was closely connected with many of the local county families. Indeed, it may be said of practically all the incumbents onwards from the Reformation to the middle of the last century that weighty local connections were their chief passport to preferment. A mournful interest attaches to his successor, Henry Eusticke. He came of the old Cornish family of Eusticke, of Nancealvan, and had married Mary Borlase, daughter of the then vicar of Madron. He was a man of undoubted learning and literary attainments, and an acknowledged authority on the ancient Cornish language, and did much during his not very long life in collecting written fragments of the ancient tongue.* He also published after the custom of the times† a collection of verses and epigrams. Unfortunately for Henry Eusticke, he lived in different times from those of his easy-going predecessors. The age had begun to grow impatient of easy-going cultured clerical somnolence. John Wesley, like other great men, seems to have been a symptom rather than the cause of the deep spiritual ferment associated with his name. The stirrings were already in the souls of the people; all that was needed was some passing cause to set these forces in motion. If proof were needed it is only necessary to realise how incapable John Wesley found himself of guiding the movement into the rigid mould that he had designed for it. The reaper can only gather in the harvest when it is ready to his sickle: he cannot create the harvest.

I give John Wesley's experience at Breage in his own words from his diary; they do not make pleasant reading because they present the spectacle of two good men utterly incapable of understanding each other's position. " I had given no notice of my preaching here, but seeing the poor flock from every side, I could not send them away empty. So I preached at a small distance from the house and besought them to consider our Great High Priest, who is passed into the heavens, and none opened his mouth, for the lions of Breage are now changed into lambs. That they were so fierce ten years ago is no wonder, since the wretched

---

* See Jenner's "Handbook of the Cornish Language."
† See Bouse's "Collectanea."

Minister told them from the pulpit, ' Seven years before I resigned my fellowship John Wesley was expelled from the College for a base child and had been quite mazed ever since,' that all the Methodists in their private Societies put out the lights, etc., etc., with abundance more of the same kind. But a year or two since it was observed he grew thoughtful and melancholy, and about nine months ago went into his house and hanged himself."

After reading this indictment of poor Mr. Eusticke, a Fellow of his College and a learned man, one naturally asks oneself the question, who were the informants of John Wesley as to this wild tirade from the pulpit ? The writer was once informed in all good faith by an old woman that a clerical neighbour in a former parish, given to preaching on Christian evidences, had stated from the pulpit his belief " That there was no God at all, and that he would never get her to hold such a belief." The writer is inclined to put these two statements in the same category, whilst attributing them perhaps to a very different attitude of mind. With all his saintly enthusiasm, John Wesley seems to have been, like many other saintly men, of a somewhat credulous disposition ; and his attributing the death of Mr. Eusticke to the fact that he opposed himself to him, to say the least, suggests a somewhat unbalanced condition of mind.

On the other hand, to the latitudinarian and philosophic Henry Eusticke, John Wesley would no doubt appear as a lawless and erratic High Church Clergyman, who out of pure self-will, in defiance of the orders of his Bishop, went about obtruding himself into parishes where he had no jurisdiction, and generally turning the world upside down. It was enthusiasm, however, and not cold moralities, coupled with a Dr. Panglos attitude towards all constituted things, as making for the best of all possible worlds, that was going to change the hearts of the people. The pity of it all is that the mutual prejudices between John Wesley and his brother clergy ended in one more cruel rent in the seamless garb of the Church—in making the holiest aspirations of the human heart, which should have been the chiefest strength of the Church, into a source of discord and division.

In speaking of John Wesley one is naturally reminded of another saintly character, the tenderest episodes in whose career are closely bound up with the parish of Breage. John Wesley confined his labours to people of his own race and language ; Henry Martyn sought to become the Apostle of India and Persia. The connection of Henry Martyn with Breage was due to Lydia Grenfell, the lady to whom he was engaged, having made her home to a large extent with her brother-in-law, a Mr. Wylliams, who for many years acted as curate-in-charge of Breage, for a non-resident pluralist incumbent. Henry Martyn thus came to pass many happy days in what is now the old Vicarage at Breage, previous to his departure for India. In his diary he pathetically tells us how he proposed spending the last Sunday in England at St. Hilary with Lydia Grenfell, but early in the morning of that day a messenger arrived from Falmouth with the news that the troopship in which he was sailing was about to put to sea with all possible speed. He immediately started from St. Hilary by road, passing through Breage on his way. There is a touching pathos in the statement in his diary that he anxiously waited on deck till the ship in which he sailed passed the Lizard Point, that he might search the twilight coast for the familiar landmarks linked with the tenderest associations of his life—one of the most prominent of which would be the old grey tower of Breage Church, visible on clear days far out to sea—but, alas ! as the ship rounded the Lizard the whole coast lay embedded in thick banks of cloud, and as the darkness fell and the ship forged out to sea this lonely pioneer of the faith descended to his cabin, and poured out his soul in prayer, that in the distant East, to which he was voyaging, he might win

kingdoms for Christ. This first of the great modern English
Missionaries was never fated to see the home of his youth
again ; his lot was not to win kingdoms for Christ, but to
find a martyr's grave in Persia. Lydia Grenfell rests at
Breage under the shadow of the old grey Church on the hill
overlooking the sea.

With the death of the second Earl of Godolphin in the
middle of the eighteenth century, rank and fashion took
leave of the parish of Breage, and the chief events in its
annals became in the future mining speculations, with
occasional wrecks and alarms of invasion.

During the summer months, in the time of Sidney
Godolphin, Godolphin House had been the constant rendezvous of the leading families of the County, and a great
centre of social life. The great Minister whilst in residence
at Godolphin had relays of messengers, who brought on his
despatches from Exeter—as far as that town they seem to
have been entrusted to the ordinary post ; in those days, it
may be added, no regular post linked Cornwall with London,
Exeter being the extreme postal limit of the West. To
Godolphin House, therefore, during the short residences of
the Lord High Treasurer of England, came men in search of
the crumbs of patronage that fell from the Minister's table, or
to hear news of the outer world, or of what transpired at Court
and who was likely to succeed on the Queen's demise, and
how it fared with Marlborough in the great war, many no
doubt of the varied throng having relatives serving under
him.

During the Napoleonic wars a Signalling Station was
established on Tregoning Hill, and anxious watch kept over
the seaward horizon for French Fleets which never hove in
sight, whilst tradition says rumours of invasion from time to
time stirred the public mind to fear.

But the real events in the sequestered life of the
district, beyond the mere fluctuations in the prosperity of

the tin trade, which stirred the pulses of public interest
were the harvest of shipwrecks which the winter storms
yielded each year to the inhabitants. The merits and values
of the cargoes of the different wrecks were never-failing topics
of interest round the firesides, memories of which still linger
in the minds of the aged. The invention of steam told sadly
against the value of this annual winter harvest : now it is
steam and steam trawlers that ruin the local fishing
industry, then it was steam striking a death blow at the local
industry of wrecking. Old men have told the writer a
legend, told to them by men of a still older generation, of
one of the first steamers to appear on the coast. The inhabitants concluded with regard to it that it was a ship on fire,
and consequently followed it in ever increasing numbers
along the coast, anxious to participate in the good things
in the hold of the ship when her crew beaten by the
flames drove her on shore. The establishment of the Wolf
Lighthouse within comparatively recent years, the fitful
gleam of whose red eye is clearly visible from our shores
far out to sea, has practically brought to an end the dismal
tale of wrecks and drowned sailors that each year produced.
Until well on into the last century it was the custom to bury
drowned sailors in trenches along the shore ; the place where
a number of these unfortunate mariners lie heaped together
in one common burial, without religious rites, is still marked
by the broken conformation of the ground. From the fact
that drowned mariners and voyagers received this unhonoured
sepulture, our Church Burial Registers are of no avail as
a guide to the history of the innumerable wrecks on our six
miles strip of coast. Not till after 1850 do we find any
record of the burial of those cast up by the sea in the
Churchyard.

The Church Registers for the year 1867 record one of
those tragedies of the sea, shrouded in mystery which can
never be unravelled. In the failing light of the evening of

the 7th January of that year, in the midst of a heavy gale, a large sailing ship was seen off the coast at Rinsey by several people ; the gathering darkness soon shrouded her from the eyes of the few watchers. She was never seen again, next morning the shore was strewn with wreckage and with dead, but no fragment bearing the name of the ill-fated ship was ever found. She had evidently struck on a reef of rocks a mile or so from the coast, only to slip off them during the wild, tempestuous night and to disappear in the depths of the sea. This ship was evidently a foreign one, as most of the drowned were of dark and swarthy appearance.

After a valued incumbency of nearly forty years, the Reverend Maurice Pridmore was succeeded in 1889 by the Reverend Jocelyn Barnes, who, with self-denying generosity, set about the restoration of Breage and Germoe Churches. The work was taken in hand almost immediately after Mr. Barnes' arrival, and was carried to its completion by Mr. Barnes at great personal cost to himself. In this labour of love he was greatly assisted by the eighth Duke of Leeds, the heir of the ancient House of Godolphin, and the Right Honourable W. H. Smith, through whose instrumentality he had been appointed to the living, whilst the Parishioners and Landowners assisted in the good work according to their several abilities. Dilapidations in the fabrics of both Churches were carefully renovated, and the beautifully-carved oak screen and reredos placed in Breage Church. The reredos was the work of Belgian artists, and like the screen is composed of oak, whilst the carved figures which adorn it are of lime wood. The central group of figures represents the adoration of the Magi ; in this group appear the figures of St. Breaca, St. Germoe and St. Corentine, the patron Saint of Cury, who is said to have been the first Bishop of Cornwall ; the carved figures on either side of this main group represent St. Peter, St. Paul, St. Anselm and St. John the Baptist, each with their appropriate emblem; beneath these figures, each in its separate niche, are the beautifully carved figures of the four Evangelists, two on either side. On the screen, amongst numerous emblems of a religious character, occurs the Godolphin crest, with the Cornish motto of the family, "*Frank ha leal ettoge,*" linked with the motto of the saintly Margaret Godolphin, "*Un Dieu un amy.*"

The fragments of ancient glass, which, as previously stated, were found in the walled-up staircase leading to the rood loft, were once more placed in the windows after having been carefully pieced together. It was also during the restoration that the frescos adorning the walls of the Church were discovered, hidden beneath successive layers of white-wash that had accumulated upon them during the course of centuries. The figures represented in the frescos are St. Christopher, bearing the infant Christ upon his shoulder, a large figure of our Lord with the crown of thorns, whilst the drops of blood caused by it are falling upon the instruments of daily village life and husbandry, thus symbolising that the business and tasks of our daily lives are blessed and sanctified by our Lord's sacrifice, and that no human work is too lowly to be recognised by the Saviour of the world; the two foregoing figures are in a wonderful state of preservation, whilst the other figures, which practically cover the walls of the body of the Church, and are in a more or less faded and obliterated condition, consist of representations of St. Hilary, St. Ambrose, St. Corentine, St. Michael, St. Giles, St. Germoe and St. Thomas of Canterbury.

At the time of the restoration, in making certain necessary excavations, large numbers of human bones in extremely shallow graves were discovered all over the interior of the Church. One large vault was found in the nave, a little in front of the site of the present pulpit, quite empty save for a handful of bones. This vault was about seven feet deep. All the remains found beneath the flooring of the Church were carefully buried under the superintendence of Mr. Barnes in this empty vault beneath a large cross of flowers ; the vault was then carefully covered over with concrete. Amongst the bones deposited in this receptacle were the six skeletons mentioned in a former chapter, which were found lying side by side, their skulls perforated with bullet wounds.

In 1910 Mrs. Cornelia Carter, of Philadelphia, U.S.A., placed a clock in the Church tower to the memory of her husband, Mr. William Thornton Carter, who, leaving Breage as a comparatively poor lad, rose to a position of great wealth in America. In his latter years his memory often turned with affection to the far-off Cornish home of his youth, and he used to speak fondly of the old village Church with its far reaching view over the waters of the Atlantic, under the shadow of whose grey tower he passed as a little lad each morning on his way to school. At the same time were placed in the Church three windows to different members of the Carter family.

The gifts of the Carter family to the Church stirred the parishioners to the putting in order of the huge single bell, the largest in Cornwall, which had long hung mute in the belfry. The quaint motto " *Complures populo, suppetit una Deo*," runs round the base of the bell, with the date of its casting in 1771. This motto may be roughly translated " The people desire many bells, but one suffices God." This curious motto supplies a hint at the cause of the casting of this bell ; the event happened during the incumbency of the Reverend Edward Marshall. It seems that it was the custom of those days for the bell ringers of the neighbouring village Churches to exchange visits of friendly rivalry. On these occasions quantities of strong waters found their way into the belfries, and their fumes into the brains of the ringers, with the result that the bells

" In the startled ear of night,
Too much horrified to speak
They can only shriek, shriek,
　　Out of tune :
Leaping, higher, higher, higher,
With a desperate desire,
And a resolute endeavour,
Now, now, to sit or never,
　　By the side of the pale-faced moon.
Oh the bells, bells, bells !
What a tale their terror tells,
　　Of despair !
How they clang and clash and roar !
What a horror they outpour
　　On the bosom of the palpitating air ! "

On one of these uproarious occasions the tenor bell broke away from its fastenings, and instead of sitting by the pale-faced moon, it came crashing through the belfry floor on to the flags at the base of the tower, nearly annihilating in the process some of the exuberant ringers. The nocturnal clash and roar seems, if tradition speaks true, to have frequently lasted all through the night. On New Year's Eve especially it was the custom to continue ringing the bells through the majority of the hours of darkness that remained after midnight. There being no regulations as to the hour of closing public houses in those days, on these occasions of festivity they remained open until all hours of the morning, and strong waters thus passed freely between the public house and the belfry, the distance being so short between them. The endless jangle of the midnight bells, it is said, got on the nerves of the Reverend Edward Marshall ; more possibly his sense of decency and fitness was stirred by these wild doings. To remedy the evil he took the drastic action of melting the four mediæval bells down into the present big one on the fall of the tenor bell from its fastening in the tower, much against the wishes of his parishioners, as the motto round the base of the bell more than hints. The process of recasting took place in the large field on the south side of the Church. This drastic operation only seems to have made matters worse, as on the following New Year's Eve, a lusty band of Tinners took possession of the belfry, and the awful " boom," " boom " of the big bell, in ceaseless iteration, sounded out over land and sea, banishing sleep through the livelong night from all within easy distance of Breage Church Tower.

We may remark that Edward Marshall was a Fellow of Exeter College, Oxford, and son of the Reverend William Marshall, of Ashprington, Devonshire. His wife was a member of the Sandys family, of Lanarth, and his grandson long represented Taunton in Parliament.

The Germoe bells were purchased by public subscription and placed in Germoe Church in 1753. The tenor bell, weighing 7 cwt., merely records the names of Edward Collins, vicar, and Samuel Lemon and Simon Harry, Churchwardens; the second bell weighs $5\frac{1}{2}$ cwt., and has engraved upon it " Prosperity to this parish." The treble bell, weighing $4\frac{1}{2}$ cwt., records the fact that " Abraham Rudhall caste us all." The Communion plate both at Breage and Germoe was the gift of Dr. Godolphin, Dean of St. Paul's; he was the brother of the great Sidney Godolphin. The plate in all consists of three very large silver-gilt flagons, two cups, one large silver paten and two small ones; these bear the date 1692. The entry recording the gift which appears in the Church registers runs as follows : " The gift of plate to our parish by Dr. Henry Godolphin and the Communion table railed in, in the year of our Lord Christ, 1693, Richard Carleen."

The registers date from 1559, but contain a number of breaks, the largest of which naturally begins with the latter years of the Protectorate, and for some unexplained reason continues well on into the reign of Charles II. The registers make it clear that at the time of their commencement there were still a number of people living in this remote corner of the West without any surname at all ; such entries as "Wilhelmus servus Wilhelmi Polkynhorne," "Johes servus Stepeni Treworlis," and "Margareta filia Thoms Robert," are all culled from the first page of the burial register. Gradually at this period the Christian names of the fathers were being adopted by the sons as surnames. The surnames Richards, Edwards, James, Thomas, Johns, Williams, Stephens were thus evolved ; Richards or Williams being in the first instance mere abbreviations of the possessive form, son of Richard or son of William ; quite ninety per cent. of the surnames in the parish fall under this head.

The great majority of the surnames in the parish which have not been formed in the foregoing way were in their original form local place names. The entry "Johes servus Stepheni Treworlis," given in the preceding paragraph, gives us an example of the method of their adoption ; the descendants of Stephen Treworlis in succeeding generations, as the registers show, being grouped under the names of Stephens or Treworlis, no doubt as chance or fancy had decided.

The following extracts from the registers recording either the marriage or deaths of the persons mentioned bring out another curious factor in the formation of local surnames, "Jo Brown, alias Uninformed," "Thomas Sampson, alias Cunning Boy," "John Arthur, alias Plain Dealing " ; these entries all occur previous to 1696 ; at later dates we have "Jane the daughter of Edmund the Tod-stoole," "Thomas, alias Punch of Germoe." Scattered through the registers we also find the elegant aliases " Two Suppers," " Stink," " Ginger," " Dissembler," " Onwise." A series of entries dating from 1713 show us how these nicknames in the course of time crystallized into actual surnames. In 1713 we have the entry " Nicholas Cornish, alias Cold Pye," in the following year he is mentioned as Nicholas Cornish

Coldpy, whilst in later years he figures in the registers simply as Nicholas Colpy. It is interesting to speculate upon the attempts at derivation that an antiquary or genealogist not knowing the true facts might devise as an explanation of the surname " Colpy."

A further curious instance of the method of the formation of local surnames is vouchsafed in our rather common surname " Meagor." The earliest form of this name in the registers is " Meneager," *e.g.* " Avis filia Thoms Meñeager, 1579," or in plain English, " Avis the daughter of Thomas of the Meneage District."

The earlier Breage registers contain here and there surnames that are not of local origin, and which savour of romance and adventure in lives long since folded in utter oblivion. In 1511 I find the death of Hugh Grymme de Godolphin recorded, in 1600 the marriage of Edmundus Erasmus, and a little later on one William Delaregetto is laid to rest at Breage, whilst the name of Angus Macdonald appears in the Germoe registers after the Forty Five.

The story of Hugh Grymme or Graeme is not difficult to piece together in its main outlines without being too fanciful. The wanderings of this northern Ulysses from the home of his clan on the shores of the Solway would make an interesting Odyssey, could they be distilled from the mists of the past. One sees the vague outline of it all fitfully. His fellow Borderers at this time,—the Armstrongs, the Elliots, the Ridleys and a hundred others—were sadly realizing that times had changed since Flodden Field, that ceaseless Border strife was coming to an end, that law was beginning to grow stronger in its grasp, and that raids and forays and cattle-lifting expeditions were each year becoming accompanied more and more with such unpleasant and undignified incidents as hangings at Jedburgh and Carlisle. For such roystering blades it was impossible to hang spear, sword, helmet and breastplate for ever to rust upon the wall, and to sink down into the life of dull tillers of the soil. There was nothing else for them to do than to troop off to the Irish wars, where they could raid and harry and slaughter the Irish to their hearts' content, all in the name of good Queen Bess, and not in defiance of her Wardens of the Marches. Many of these riders of the Borders founded families in Ireland, and came to own broad acres, and many no doubt found nameless graves. Hugh Graeme, it would seem probable, was one of these Border adventurers who found neither wealth nor a grave in Ireland, but service with Sir William Godolphin, who had spent his youth fighting under Essex in Ireland. No doubt Hugh Graeme had ridden behind Sir William in his campaigns, often with death on his saddle bow, and when fighting days were over came with his master to Godolphin, where Death, who had passed him by in the wars, found him and claimed him.

The name Erasmus twice occurs in the Breage registers, and in the next generation makes its appearance in the guise of " Rasmus." In 1660 the marriage of Edmundus Erasmus is recorded with Johanna Caraver. I cannot think that in this case Erasmus is a mere second Christian name, because shortly after we have the baptism entry " Thomas Erasmus," and in 1687 we have the marriage entry " Joisea Rasmus." Nor do I think it probable that the surname Erasmus, as it occurs in the Breage registers, grew out of a Christian name given in the first instance on account of its popularity with Reformers, because in this case the registers would have shewn some trace of Erasmus used as a Christian name, which they do not.

The appearance of this name in the registers tallies with the great activity of Sir Francis Godolphin in developing the tin mines upon his estates. Under the circumstances it seems probable that Edmundus Erasmus was one of the Continental experts whom we know that he employed in improving the local methods of mining ; this conclusion, however, in no way elucidates the mystery that clings round the name. The great humanist namesake of Edmundus. who died in 1536, was, like many of the Cornish tinners, born without a surname, his father only possessing the Christian name of Gerhard, of which Erasmus is meant to be the Greek rendering. We may therefore very well conclude that no other surname of Erasmus existed in the world, save that of the great humanist, and that it must have begun and ended with him, because as a priest he could have had no legitimate issue. On the other hand, I cannot think that anyone would adopt Erasmus as a surname having absolutely no connection in blood with the great Dutch scholar. Here we have one of those strange and often fascinating mysteries with which the registers of our parishes abound. Their yellow pages so often, like withered rose leaves, suggest the joy, the youth, the sunlight and the tragedy of forgotten summers.

In 1686 we find the marriage entry of William Dellaregetto, and in 1730 the entry of the marriage of Zenobia Dellaregetto. The name Dellaregetto certainly suggests the sunny skies of Italy, whilst Angus Macdonald conjures up a vision of the Scottish Highlands. Possibly the first Dellaregetto may have been some Italian sailor cast away upon our shores. From a descendant of Angus Macdonald, still living in the parish, I have been able to obtain a fleeting glimpse of the story of this man. He arrived (I imagine on board some smuggling craft) about one hundred and fifty years ago, and settled for a year or two at Rinsey and went through the ceremony of marriage with a Breage woman, after having been a resident at Rinsey for some little time. Tradition says that he was a person with plenty of money, and a man of high station in his own country, and that at the close of the wars a price was set upon his head by the Government. If tradition speaks true it seems probable, considering the date of his coming, that this Macdonald was a man of some importance, who had been out in the Forty Five,—possibly some minor chief of the clan Macdonald. He disappeared as suddenly as he came, whether to his native land on having made his peace with the Government, or, as is more probable, to join his exiled compatriots in France or Spain, where life was less dull, who can say? At any rate, his Cornish wife and children saw and heard of him no more. His descendants are still living in the parish.

Perhaps the following curious entry from the registers may be of interest to the reader : " Thomas Epsley, senior, of Chilchampton, parish of Bath and Wells, Summersitsheers ; he was the man who brought here the rare invention of shooting the rocks, which came here in June, 1689, and he died at the Bal and was buried at Breag, the 16th day of December, in the yeare of Our Lord Christ, 1689." Subsequent entries in the burial register make it clear that "the rare invention of shooting the rocks" i.e. blasting, was anything but an unmixed blessing to those who had to apply it to the rocks.

I find in the registers the record of a great snowstorm in December, 1630, in which four persons perished, and another at the end of January and the beginning of February, 1692. To these great snowstorms may well be added that of March, 1891, which not only isolated the parish from the rest of the world, but the householders from each other, save in the village and hamlets, for several days. This terrible storm also levied from the parish its toll of human life.

The following grim entry from the burial register, bearing date 2nd February, 1693, illustrates the methods and views of a former age, which seem strangely out of touch with our own : " Samuel Rogers, of Crava, being excommunicate, was laid in the earth in the Church at night."

I find in the registers the records of but few briefs. At Germoe in 1682 five shillings was collected for the

"distressed Protestants of France," and in the same year ten
shillings for the sufferers in the great fire at the town of
Cullompton in Devonshire. At Breage I only find records
of briefs in the year 1712; they were for the restoration of
Battle Bridge, West Tilbury and St. Clement's Church,
presumably of this diocese.

It is to be regretted that the churchwardens' accounts
have long since, through damp and neglect, passed beyond
the stage when it is possible to examine them. The Parish
Councils Act with all its benefits committed a terrible
mistake in consigning the ancient records of the Church
Vestries, in many cases going back for hundreds of years, to
the custody of simple, well-meaning but unlettered men, with
no realisation of the value of ancient documents. Too often
they have been jumbled into an old wooden box in a
damp vestry room, and left to grow green with mould and
disintegrate into an evil-smelling paste; at least such is
an instance in the writer's experience. In another case,
the fountain of village wisdom informed a learned antiquary
that he could not be allowed to inspect their documents;
whilst in a third case the clerk to a Parish Council parted
with an ancient document, that had come down through
the generations with the Church Vestry papers, to an
old gentleman who was in the habit of shewing it to his friends
as a curiosity. · On the death of the old gentleman in question
a friend of the writer, in the hope that the document might
prove of interest, and that he might be able to return it to
the vicar of the parish from whence it had been originally
taken, endeavoured to purchase it from the heir, when it
transpired that the document had been burnt as waste paper.

The following items from the Breage churchwardens'
accounts I have been able to cull from a note-book of the
Reverend Jocelyn Barnes. Whilst of no paramount importance, they serve as vivid illustrations of the dead-and-gone
life of the village.

"1774—Mr. John Hood and Company for Oilcloth Umbrella for the Parson at funerals," £1 0s. 6d.

1772—For the charge of prosecuting against the Kitows for the murder of Henry Thomas, junior, as per bill of particulars, £18 4s. 2d.

1797—Feb. 2nd, to a new white sheet for William Fischer to do penance, 6d. ; ditto, to the expense of the occasion, one shilling.

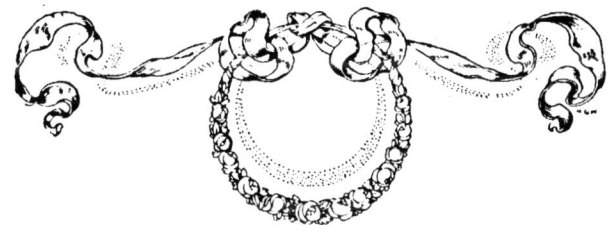

THE GODOLPHINS.

CHAPTER VI.

The family of Godolphin is by far the greatest and most important that has issued from our parish. Their original abode, according to the statement of Leland, was a fortified stronghold or tower on Godolphin Hill, the remains of which were in existence in his time. The origin of the family is lost in obscurity, but the curious tenure under which the Manor of Godolphin is still held from the owner of the Manor of Lambourne makes it clear that they were not tenants-in-chief from the Earls of Cornwall. A passing allusion to the curious nature of this tenure may be pardoned. Each Candlemas morning at six o'clock, beneath the twinkling stars, or more probably in the black darkness of rain and tempest, the Reeve of Lambourne still pays his yearly visit to Godolphin House. Beating on the outer oaken doors of

Godolphin House.

the ancient mansion, he peremptorily demands admission. On the doors being opened, without waiting for invitation he enters the house and mounting upon the table of the hall he exclaims "O Yes! O Yes! O Yes! I am the Reeve of Lambourne in Perransand, come here to demand the old rent, duties and customs due to the lords of the said manor from the lands of Godolphin." In response to the summons of the Reeve there is brought him 2s. 8d. in rent, a jack of strong beer, a loaf of bread and a cheese. Out of the fact of this ancient tenure the incorrigible Hals has woven one of his innumerable romances, for which not one iota of evidence worthy of consideration exists. Hals possessed the art of evolving history of a libellous and defamatory character from his own inner consciousness in a way that has been seldom equalled.

After a number of generations the ancient race of Godolphin centred in an heiress Elinor or Elianora, who married John Rinsey of Rinsey, thus joining the estates of Rinsey and Godolphin. On 2nd December, 1398, John Rinsey of Godolphin and Rinsey and Elianora his wife received a licence from Bishop Stafford for oratories on their manors of Godolphin and Rinsey. The arms of this worthy pair are still to be seen quartered on the 15th century screen of Buryan Church.

Hals' story about the Godolphin estates passing by marriage to the Arundells of Perransand, and being sold to one Stephens or Knava, on the above-mentioned tenure, rests upon no proof save that the name of Knava happened to be common in Breage in his time, and it finds no support from the descent of the family given by Vivian.

John Godolphin of Godolphin, Sheriff of Cornwall in 1504, must be regarded as the real John of Hapsbourg of his race. I am led to conclude that the Master Thomas Godolphin who became vicar of Breage in 1505 was the younger son of this founder of the family greatness.

The south-east corner of Breage Church, now called the

Godolphin Chapel, was the burying-place of this ancient family from the period of its rise to greatness, though no monument of any kind preserves the memory of those whose earthly remains rest there. It seems incredible that no monuments to the memory of departed Godolphins ever marked the site of their last resting-place. Sir Francis Godolphin, who lived in the time of Elizabeth, was a man of vast wealth, as well as vast influence. The age of Elizabeth was an age of ornate and magnificent tombs ; they still survive in great numbers in our country churches, of elaborate character with rows of kneeling figures and inscriptions that will suggest the lines :

"The sculptor's art exhausts the pomp of woe,
And storied urns record who rests below ;
When all is done upon the tomb is seen
Not what he was, but what he should have been."

The conclusion is forced upon us that at some period the tombs of the Godolphins were removed and desecrated. As to the period there can be little doubt ; it can only be placed in the time of the Independent ascendancy, during the Protectorate. The Godolphins had distinguished themselves by their fearless loyalty to the exiled house, and had rendered themselves a target for the animosity of the Government and local fanatics and sectaries. Their elaborate tombs were thus perhaps conveniently confused with the emblems of superstition, and their recesses rifled in search of sacrilegious booty.

The helmets of three Godolphins still hang in the southeast corner of the church, the silken banners that once hung with them having long since mouldered into dust. At the restoration of the church in 1892 two large marble slabs were removed from the floor of the church, which marked the stairway leading to the Godolphin vault. John Evelyn, in his account of the burial of Margaret Godolphin, speaks of this quiet corner as the "dormitorie of her family."

A Godolphin Helmet in Breage Church.

Sir John Godolphin was succeeded by his son, Sir William Godolphin ; this Knight in his turn was repeatedly Sheriff of Cornwall. We may gather from the State Papers* that his character and principles, to say the least, were somewhat robust. Ships cast upon the wild, rockbound coast of Breage, it is complained, were snapped up as toothsome morsels by the Sheriff, and their contents carried doubtless as loot to Godolphin. His burial is recorded in the Breage register on 30th July, 1570. He was succeeded by his son, the heroic Sir

---

*State Papers, 1526.

William Godolphin, who covered himself with glory in the short war waged by Henry VIII. against Francis I., which terminated in the defeat of the French at the Battle of the Spurs. Carew says of this brave Knight that "he added lustre to his fame at the expense of his face." This statement has reference to a charge made by Sir William and his brother Thomas, at the head of the force under his command, which resulted in the route of the French opposed to them and the grievous shortening of Sir William's nose by a sword cut. This warrior at home seems to have practised the robust methods of his father. In 1575 we find the *Crown preferring fifteen charges against him, thirteen of which were for piracy in conjunction with the Killigrews of Arwennick. He lies buried in Finchley Churchyard, and some faithful follower who had wandered over the fields of Picardy with him in search of military glory placed the following epitaph upon his tomb :

"Godolphin his race to rest hath run,
  Where grace affords felicity ;
  His death is gone, his life hath wone
  Eternal perpetuity.
  Though William his corpse here doth lie
  Barnes' faith in him shall never die."

His wife Dame Blanche Godolphin lies at Breage. As Sir William left no son his estates devolved on his nephew, Sir Francis, son of Thomas Godolphin, who had, as we have already seen, distinguished himself in the war with France. Of Sir Francis Godolphin, Carew says, "Zeal in religion, uprightness in government and plentifulness in house-keeping had given him a great reputation."

As well as having distinguished himself in the dreary wars of Ireland, Sir Francis had applied his mind to the problems of scientific mining on his estates, to his own great profit.

---

* State Papers.

In looking over the pages of the Church registers, I was perplexed to find the frequent recurrence of the name Erasmus. There can be but little doubt that the first Erasmus, whose name appears in the registers was a Dutchman brought to Breage by Sir Francis Godolphin in connection with his great projects of scientific mining. Sir Francis was Governor of the Scilly Islands. As Governor he rebuilt the ruined fortress of St. Mary, and made it so strong that it successfully resisted all the assaults of the Parliamentary forces until the close of the Civil War. The heroic attempt of Sir Francis Godolphin to defend Penzance against the attacking Spaniards has been dealt with in another place.

Sir Francis corresponded with Cecil Lord Burleigh, and we thus get from the Hatfield MS. a faint, blurred picture of the soul of this brave Cornish squire. In his last letter to Cecil, dated Tavistock, 8th October, 1601, he speaks of his " project as touching the wars in Ireland."[*] He married first Margaret, daughter of John Killigrew, of Arwenack, and secondly Alice, daughter of John Skerrit, and widow of John Glanville, Judge of the Court of Common Pleas. Of one of these ladies the following quaint story still survives : Sir Francis had taken into his confidence an attorney of Ottery St. Mary, named John Cole, and ultimately employed him as his agent. This person embarked in mining speculations on his own account with disastrous results, which soon hurried him into the paths of fraud. John Cole's blocks of tin bore for purposes of identification the figure of a cat stamped upon them, whilst those of his master bore the impress of a dolphin. Emboldened by successful peculations, the sign of the cat appeared in ever-increasing numbers where the sign of the dolphin should have been displayed. The suspicions of Lady Godolphin, more shrewd in this respect than her husband, were aroused. Accom-

---

[*] See "The Life of Sidney Godolphin," by the Hon. Hugh Eliot.

panied by a maid, she repaired to the Godolphin Blowing House on foot, where she found numerous blocks of tin unlawfully stamped with the sign of the cat. On her return to Godolphin House, she found Sir Francis and a number of friends wondering at her absence, prolonged long past the appointed hour of dinner. She explained that during her absence she "had been watching a cat eating a dolphin." The Breage registers record the burial of Sir Francis Godolphin on 23rd April, 1608.

Sir Francis was succeeded by his son, Sir William Godolphin, educated at Emmanuel College, Cambridge, the home in those days of Puritan learning. Sir William also had distinguished himself under Essex in Ireland ere he succeeded his father ; tradition says that he had been knighted for his bravery on the field of battle. In 1606 he was employed by the Government on a mission to Paris, the object of which is unknown. In an extant letter to Cecil[*] he complains that his means were inadequate to meet the expenses of the mission. He represented Cornwall once, if not twice, in Parliament. He married Thomasina, the daughter of Thomas Sidney, of Wrighton, in Norfolk. It was thus that the Christian name of Sidney was introduced into the Godolphin family. The Breage registers record his burial on 5th September, 1613. His eldest son William died whilst still a youth, when on a visit to Bruton Abbey, in Somersetshire ; he was thus succeeded by his second son Francis, a boy of fourteen at the time of his father's death.

It was during the lifetime of this Sir Francis that Charles II., then Prince of Wales, took refuge at Godolphin House, on his flight to the Scilly Islands on the complete collapse of the Royal cause. Charles remembered the services of his faithful Cornish squire, and at his accession made him a Knight of the Bath, and entrusted to his charge the State

---

[*] See "The Life of Sidney Godolphin," by the Hon. Hugh Eliot.

prisoners, Sir Harry Vane and General Ireton ; at the same time the foundation of the fortunes of his third son, Sidney, was laid by admission to the Royal household. Sir Francis represented St. Ives and other constituencies in Parliament. He and his wife, Dame Dorothy, daughter of Sir Henry Berkeley, of Yarlington in Somerset, were both buried in Breage Church. Sir Francis was succeeded by his eldest son, Sir William, who died without issue, and is buried at Breage. His fourth son, Henry Godolphin, D.D., was Provost of Eton for thirty-five years, and ultimately became Dean of St. Paul's. The silver-gilt Communion services still in use at both the Churches of Breage and Germoe were the gift of Henry Godolphin, whilst Dean of St Paul's. The record of his baptism occurs in our registers on 15th August, 1648.

No account of the house of Godolphin would be complete without mention of the brave and debonair Sidney Godolphin, poet, soldier and philosopher, brother of the foregoing Sir Francis Godolphin, K.B. He was the trusted friend of the statesman Clarendon, Hobbes the philosopher, and Waller the Cavalier poet. These three friendships in themselves made clear the temper of his mind. He sat in three Parliaments as member for Helston. He espoused in Parliament the cause of Strafford, and when peace seemed hopeless, he withdrew to the King at Oxford. The Earl of Clarendon in his history of the Great Rebellion has left a vivid portrait of his character and personality. He describes him as of small stature, but of sharp and keen wit, with a mind tinged with melancholy and fitfulness. He tells us that he would scarcely stir out of doors in windy or rainy weather, and that at Court he mingled freely with the greatest of the realm. He died fighting for his King at Chagford, in Devonshire, in an obscure skirmish, and lies buried in Okehampton Parish Church. It is evident that he had inherited the nature of his mother, and was a Sidney both in mind and in person rather than a Godolphin. Sidney

Godolphin was before his age, and his philosophic mind revolted at the miserable tangle of religion and politics, and the degrading spirit of religious intolerance and persecution manifested by all parties. Of him it might have been well said : " *Qui n'as pas l'esprit de son âge, de son âge a tout le malheur.*" On his tomb are inscribed the following pathetic lines by his friend Hobbs :

" Thou art dead, Godolphin, who lov'dst reason true,
Justice and peace, soldier belov'd, adieu."

The following entry in the Breage registers, which casts a sidelight on the story of the Godolphin family, has a pathos all its own : " Franciscus Berkeley, filius Caroli Berkeley militis, sepultus fuit 27 Septembri, 1635." The mother of the child whose death is thus recorded was Penelope, daughter of Sir William Godolphin, and the sister of Sir Francis and Sidney Godolphin. Penelope Godolphin had been married to Sir Charles Berkeley in Breage Church, September, 1627. Possibly the rapid rise of the Godolphin family was due to some extent to this marriage into the powerful family of Berkeley. Sir Charles Berkeley afterwards became Viscount Hardinge, and ultimately Earl of Falmouth, and is said in the main to have been responsible for the failure of the negotiations between Cromwell and Ireton on the one hand, and Charles I. on the other, for the restoration of Charles once more, to a peaceful, if a more limited authority over his people.

The child whose death the entry records had doubtless come with his parents to his mother's ancestral home. Penelope Berkeley no doubt returned to the old home of her childhood full of dreams of the renewal of the life of her girlhood, proud of her firstborn, heir to a great name. It all ended, alas ! in the laying of the body of her babe in the old grey Church on the hill, overlooking the sea, 'midst the dust of his maternal ancestors.

The parish has produced only one great man of the first

rank, Sidney Godolphin, Earl of Godolphin, third son of the Sir Francis honoured by Charles II. Our Church registers record the baptism of Sidney Godolphin in the following words : " Sidoni, the son of Francis Godolphin and Dorothy his wife, was baptized 15th day of June, 1644." Sidney Godolphin almost immediately after the Restoration became a page in the Royal household, and it was not long before the King conceived a strong personal liking for the son of the Cornish squire with whom he had found a refuge in the darkest hour of his fortunes. The regard of the merry Monarch made smooth the path of rapid advancement for Sidney Godolphin. Like his uncle of the same name, at an early age he entered Parliament as member for Helston. It is said that he very seldom spoke in the House of Commons, but quickly earned a reputation as a man of keen financial grasp and insight, and that his opinion on matters of finance soon came to be regarded as of great weight. In 1679 he was promoted with Viscount Hyde, afterwards Earl of Rochester, and the Earl of Sunderland to the chief management of affairs. In September, 1684, he was created Baron Godolphin of Rialton, and succeeded the Earl of Rochester as First Lord of the Treasury. James II. extended to him the same favour and confidence that King Charles had given to him. He was one of the Council of Five to whom James left the management of affairs when he left London to meet the advancing forces of the Prince of Orange. On the utter collapse of the cause of James II. he was one of the Commissioners appointed to negotiate with William Prince of Orange. He continued in office under William III., whilst at the same time, like his friend the Duke of Marlborough, he carried on a secret correspondence with James at St. Germans. No doubt all his real sympathies were with the cause of the exiled Monarch. In the reign of Anne he was largely instrumental in bringing about the Act of Union with Scotland ; and by his great ability as a Minister of Finance he alone rendered possible the victorious prosecution of the war with France. He was created Earl of Godolphin in 1706. His position as a Minister of Finance in a venal age gave him unlimited opportunities for peculation, which others would have unblushingly seized, but he remained incorruptible, and at his death in 1712 was found to be worth only £12,000. He was buried in Westminster Abbey.

The life of Sidney Godolphin was early clouded by a great sorrow. At the age of thirty he had married Margaret Blague, daughter of Colonel Blague, of Horningsheath. Three years after their marriage, in 1678, Margaret Godolphin's saintly life came to an end. John Evelyn has rendered the story of her short life in a sense the common heritage of all English men and women. By her purity and simple goodness of character she came to exercise an influence upon an evil and licentious Court, and for posterity she stands out as one of its brightest ornaments. I extract the following fragment from Evelyne's memoir of her : " She died in the 26 yeare of age, to the inexpressible affliction of her deare husband. She was for beauty and good nature, wit, fidelity and discretion the most incomparable person. Her husband, struck with the unspeakable affliction, fell down as dead. The King himself and all the Court expressed their sorrow. To the poore and miserable her loss was irreparable, for there was no degree but had some obligation to her memorei. She desired to be buried in the dormitorie of her husband's family, neere 300 miles from all her other friends. So afflicted was her husband at this severe loss that the entire care of her funeral was committed to me. Having close-l her eyes, and dropped a teare upon the cheeke of my deare departed friend, lovely even in death, I caused the corpse to be embalmed and wrapped in lead, with a plate of brass soldered thereon, with an inscription and other circumstances due to her worth, with as much diligence and care that my grieved heart would permit me. She was accordingly carried to

Godolphin, in Cornwall, in a hearse with six horses, attended by two coaches of as many, with about thirty of her relations and servants. There accompanied the hearse her husband's brother, Sir William, two more of his brothers and his three sisters; her husband was so overcome with grief that he was wholly unfit to travel so long a journey till he was more composed. I went as far as Hounslow with a sad heart, but was obliged to return on some indispensable affairs. The corpse was ordered to be taken out of the hearse every night, and decently placed in ye house, with tapers about it, and her servants attending to Cornwall; and then was honorably interr'd in the Parish Church of Godolphin. This funeral cost not much less than £1000. With Mr. Godolphin I looked over and sorted his lady's papers. We found a diary of her solemn resolutions, all tending to practical virtue. It astonish'd us to see what she had read and written, her youth considered."

A brass with the following inscription marks the spot in Breage Church, in front of the altar in the south aisle, beneath which the earthly remains of Margaret Godolphin lie: "Beneath this brass repose the mortal remains of Margaret Godolphin, daughter of Colonel Blague, of Hornings-heath, Groom of the Bedchamber to King Charles I.; the wife of Sidney Godolphin, afterwards Earl of Godolphin; and the friend of John Evelyn, who has told the story of her noble life. She wished to rest at Breage, the cradle of her husband's race. Born 2nd August, 1652. She died in London 9th September, 1678. This brass was placed to her memory by George Godolphin Osborne, 10th Duke of Leeds."

It seems to have been the custom of the Lord High Treasurer, at any rate until his later years, from time to time to visit his old Cornish home, which, it may be added, did not become his property until two years before his death at the decease of his elder brother in 1710.

An interesting picture of these visits has come down to

us from the father of Dr. Borlase,* of antiquarian fame, who in his youth was present on one of these occasions. He says that at this time no regular post or means of transit, either for persons or things, were to be found beyond Exeter, but when masses of letters had accumulated at Exeter they were from time to time sent on to Cornwall, as occasion might serve, by a system which was called the post. When the Lord High Treasurer, however, visited Godolphin, he had a weekly messenger from Exeter bringing letters, despatches and a newspaper ; and on the fixed day of the messenger's arrival all the gentlemen for many miles round assembled at Godolphin House to hear the newspaper read in the great hall.

A number of letters addressed to Sidney Godolphin by his mother and other members of his family still survive in the British Museum† also letters of Sidney and his sisters to their mother. These letters give a deeply interesting picture of the family life as lived at Godolphin. Some of the letters of his sisters to their mother deal with the things they saw and did on their visits to London. Money seems to have been not too abundant at this period in the Godolphin family, and considerations of ways and means constantly obtrude themselves in the letters. In one letter the future Lord High Treasurer is commissioned by his mother to purchase the wedding trousseau of one of his sisters ; to this letter of his mother the future Finance Minister replies that he has purchased the dresses that a " Mrs. Stuart had had out of France just before the Court went into mourning." This engagement between his sister Catherine and a Mr. Dryden ultimately came to naught. Catherine remained unmarried, and was the last of her line to be laid in the " dormitorie " of her race in Breage Church. She died 7th October, 1678.

Godolphin House was fitfully inhabited by Francis, 2nd Earl of Godolphin, the only son of the Lord High Treasurer, for a few summer months. He seems to have somewhat enlarged the house and built the front portico and colonnade of granite from Tregoning Hill. Since his death in 1766 this ancient house has never been inhabited by its owners, and of it may be said in the words of Hafiz :

"The spider has woven her web in the palace and the owl hath sung her watch song on the towers."

In concluding the account of the family of Godolphin, it is fitting to make some mention of Sir William Godolphin, of Treveneag, in the parish of Mabe. He was the grandson of that Sir Francis Godolphin who so gallantly attempted to defend Penzance against the Spaniards, his father being John Godolphin, Captain of the Scilly Isles. Sir William in the days of the Commonwealth had eulogised the Protector in fulsome verses still extant : when the Protector was dead, and could no longer punish or reward, we find him on the other hand assailing his memory with virulent abuse. It is only just to add that whilst singing the praises of the Protector, he was in full communication with the spies and agents of Charles. Having so carefully prepared for the future, at the Restoration his advance was rapid. In 1661 he became member of Parliament for Camelford, and spoke vehemently in favour of the sanctity of the Royal prerogative, not going without substantial reward for his exuberant loyalty. Mr. Pepys describes him as "a very pretty and able person ; a man of very fine parts." He affected science as then understood, and became a Fellow of the newly-formed Royal Society, and on account of the sunshine of the Royal favour in which he basked received the honorary degree of D.C.L. from the University of Oxford. He ultimately became Ambassador Extraordinary to the Court of Spain, but was summoned home during the frenzy of the Popish Plot on a charge of high treason. Sir William under the circumstances thought it more prudent to disregard the command and remain at Madrid as a private person, which he continued to do until the day of his death in 1696. At his death he left considerable property in Madrid, Rome, Venice and Amsterdam, which continued for a number of years to be the source of much litigation. A portion of the property was ultimately employed, in accordance with the provisions of Sir William's will, in founding the Godolphin School at Hammersmith. The Godolphin School at Salisbury, it may be added, was founded by his niece, Elizabeth Godolphin.

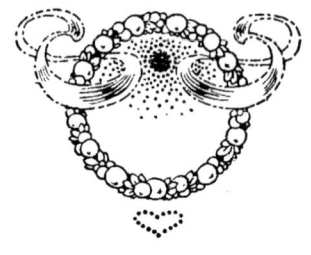

The Arundells, de Pengersicks, Militons and Sparnons.

CHAPTER VII.

At the conclusion of the Norman Conquest all the land in the parish of Breage was in the possession of the Earls of Cornwall, with the exception of the manor of Methleigh, which still continued to be attached to the See of Exeter. Methleigh passed from the Bishops of Exeter[*] to the Dean and Chapter of Exeter about 1160. Soon afterwards it was granted by the Dean and Chapter to the Nansladons, or Lansladons; from this family it passed to the Chamonds, and from them to the Arundells.

In the fifteenth century the Arundells owned the Breage manors of Pengwedna, Methleigh and Treworlas; in fact a very large section of the parish. The ancient home of this family was at Yewton, in Devonshire, where they had been settled the days of King Stephen. They are said to have been of Norman origin, and that the first form of their name was Hirondelle; at any rate, the swallow figures upon their shields. It is possible, on the other hand, that this device of the swallow may have been merely due to the vogue for canting heraldry, an example of which we have in the Godolphin helmets hanging from the roof in Breage Church, which take the form of sea monsters or dolphins rearing their heads above the waves. A more prosaic but probable origin of the Arundells would connect them with the ancient Sussex town of that name. The pathway of the Arundells to greatness[†] lay not so much by the way of the tented field as along the

---

[*] For the history of the Manor of Methleigh I am indebted to the Rev. T. Taylor, of St. Just.

[†] See Vivian's "Visitations of Cornwall," Lyson's "Cornwall," etc., etc.

flowery paths of successful match-making; they moved
forward rather to the music of wedding bells than to the
brazen blast of the trumpet sounding the charge. It was
to the former music that their broad lands in Breage came
to them.

In the thirteenth century Ralph Arundell had risen to
influence and the possession of the manors of Trembath
and Treloy through marriage with the heiress of the
Trembaths; and in the following century his descendant
acquired the manor of Lanherne by marriage with the
heiress of the ancient house of Pincerna.

The manor of Pengwedna in Breage was held by the
senior branch of the family, the Arundells of Lanherne;
whilst the manors of Treworlas and Methleigh were held by
the Arundells of Tolverne, one of the junior branches[*] of
the family. Tolverne had come to the house of Arundell in
the usual way in the reign of Richard II., Sir John Arundell
of Lanherne having married the heiress of the manor, the
daughter of Ralph le Sore. Sir John Arundell bequeathed
this estate to his second son, Thomas, whose descendants held
it until the time of Charles I. It was at Tolverne that Henry
VIII. was entertained with great magnificence by his
kinsman the Sir John Arundell of that day.

The story of the coming of the Arundells of Tolverne
to their small manor of Truthnal, in the parish of Sithney, is
full of the flavour of ancient romance. It was at the time
that the world was still dreaming of the land of El Dorado.
The spoils of Mexico and Peru brought home by the
Spaniards had profoundly moved the imaginations of all
adventurous souls. Sir Thomas Arundell, of Tolverne, had
listened to the tales of home-coming[†] adventurers of a

---

[*] Other powerful branches of the Arundell family were settled at Trerice,
Mandarva and Tremoderet, in the Parish of Duloe.

[†] See Lyson's "Cornwall."

marvellous island on the coast of America, called Old Brazil, where untold wealth lay ready as spoil for the brave and stout-hearted. He wasted his substance in vain search for this island of beauty and wealth—the pearl of American seas. Where he searched we do not know; only that his search was vain, and that he returned to his own land broken in fortune and probably also in spirit and in health, and that he was compelled to part with his ancestral acres of Tolverne and to make his home on his smaller estate in Sithney and Breage, which still remained to him from the wreck of his fortunes. He was succeeded by his son, John Arundell, who served as a Colonel of Horse in the army of the King during the Civil War. This gallant soldier was buried in the north aisle of Sithney Church, and the tablet to his memory, which takes the form of a stone shield, blazoned with swallows, is the only memorial now remaining of this once powerful family. The male line of this branch of the family became extinct on the death of John Arundell, in India, in 1776. Their estate of Methleigh was sold to the Coode family in the eighteenth century, and still continues in their possession. The manor of Treworlas which they had previously held in the parish had passed in marriage to the Jago family in the seventeenth century. The Arundells are still represented in our midst in the female line in Messrs. John Arundell and William Arundell Pryor, of Lower and Higher Pengwedna, through Margaret Arundell, who married Richard Pryor, of Sithney, in 1704.

The manor of Pengwedna remained in the family of Arundell, of Lanherne, until it was sold in the eighteenth century by Lord Arundell of Wardour, who had inherited the estates of his Cornish kinsmen.

With regard to the manor of Methleigh, it may be worthy of mention that an ancient chapel seems to have existed on this manor, close to Tremearne Farm. A carved pillar of ecclesiastical design still survives, now used as a gate-post, and from time to time carved stones have been unearthed round the spot, one, I am told, containing a realistic representation of the Crucifixion. Round the presumed site of this chapel human bones have from time to time been laid bare. I have been unable to find any record of this forgotten chapel. As the spot commands a wide view of the sea, which beats upon the rocks below, its erection may have been due to the vow of some voyager who had escaped from the fury of the waves, and the bones resting round it may be those of drowned mariners ; or it may be that we have here the site of the oratory of the ancient home of the Nansladons or the Chamonds; at any rate, all record of this ancient house of God and God's acre have long since faded into oblivion.

From the ancient family of Arundell we naturally pass to the owners of the tradition-haunted manor of Pengersick. An ancient race bearing the name of the manor long flourished there, their first coming being long since lost in the mists of the past. The Pengersicks are credited still in the minds of the people as having been remorseless wreckers, luring ships to their doom on the Sands of Praa by false lights displayed on the shore. In a persistent tradition of this kind there is as a rule a substratum of fact ; tradition has been proved time after time to rest upon a solid basis of truth, preserving for future generations a blurred vision of events from a long-forgotten past. That the Pengersicks were men of wild deeds, the assault by a member of the race, Henry de Pengersick, on David de Lyspein, Vicar of Breage, in 1335, whilst collecting the ecclesiastical dues of the parish, lends more than a suggestion ; the assault, as we have seen in a former chapter, being of such a grievous and heinous nature as to lead to Henry Pengersick being placed under the ban of excommunication.

Mr. Robert Hunt, in his " Popular Romances of the West of England," has preserved one of the wild Pengersick legends, which I venture to record in an abbreviated form. The first Pengersick, so the legend runs, was a proud man, and desired to ally himself, if possible, with one of the great families of the county. In pursuance of this purpose he

Pengersick Castle.

decided that his only son should wed a lady of high degree who was by no means young, and who had made her inclinations in the matter all too manifest. The heir of Pengersick, however, had no desire to fall in with the plans of his father and the wishes of the elderly spinster. The black witch of Fraddam was therefore consulted—a terrible old beldam versed in all manner of sorceries; but even the strongest love potions that she could brew were powerless to melt the heart of young Pengersick. Love in the heart of the spinster, subjected to constant rebuffs and coldness, began to change to hate, and his father, finding that the heart of his son was obdurate, and his nature most obstinate, made suit to the spinster of high degree himself, and was smiled upon. Now it happened that the witch of Fraddam had a niece called Bitha, who had assisted her aunt in the brewing of her unholy potions. Bitha too, like the elderly spinster—now spinster no longer—had also fallen under the spell of the manly beauty of young Pengersick, and in order to win his affections determined to take service with his stepmother, now duly ensconced in Pengersick Castle. It fell out in the course of time as Bitha had hoped, and she won young Pengersick's heart, but unfortunately their love was discovered by the harridan stepmother ; this discovery served only to deepen her hatred for one whom previously she had so passionately loved. She therefore determined once more without delay to employ the services of the black witch of Fraddam, whom she had previously discarded as an incapable physician. But here Bitha stepped in. She had not served an apprenticeship to her aunt, the witch of Fraddam, in vain ; she had kept her eyes open all the while she had helped in filling the caldron on Fraddam Down with horrible brews, and the knowledge thus obtained enabled her now to foil all the spells of her aunt upon the life of her beloved with more powerful counter-spells. At last the wicked old beldam of Pengersick, despairing once more of the weapons of sorcery, determined to arm herself with the more powerful ones of calumny and slander. She succeeded in persuading the foolish old lord, her husband, that his son was now manifesting the deepest affection towards her. This tale was altogether too much for the dotard to bear, and it stung him to ungovernable fury. He at once fell in with the carefully-prepared promptings of his wife, and had his unfortunate son seized by a gang of ruffian sailors, who carried him off to a ship that lay riding in the bay, in which he was taken to Morocco and sold as a slave. After this we gather that the poor old lord had little peace of mind ; both mistress and maid were at one in desiring his dissolution. It was not long, till sad and weary he lay a-dying, when Bitha came and stood by his bed, and with pleasing candour divested herself of the mask of kindly affection behind which she had hitherto hidden herself, and in hard staccato tones told him of the vile machinations of his wife, and that he was now dying from the effects of slow poisons, which she herself had administered to him. There was now nothing more left for the poor old lord of Pengersick to do than to wearily turn his face to the wall and die, like many before and after him to whom knowledge had come too late.

After the lapse of long years, the heir of Pengersick suddenly returned to his home, bringing with him a dusky Eastern bride, whose beauty was like a dream. He and his bride were accompanied by two swarthy servants, with whom they conversed in a strange language. The lord of Pengersick used to ride forth from the castle mounted upon a coal-black charger ; so obedient and docile in all its ways was this steed to its master that it soon came to be universally regarded as undoubtedly of satanic origin. The new lord on his return found his wicked and foolish old stepmother shut up in her chamber, with her skin covered with scales like a serpent, from the effect of the fumes of the hell-broth that she had been constantly brewing with the witch of Fraddam for his undoing and the infatuation of the foolish old lord his father. In her pain and misery she at last ridded him of her presence, and sought relief in death by plunging into the waves of the sea. The fumes of the witch's caldron, we gather, had also been too much for Bitha, and her once beautiful face had taken on the hue of a toad. She lived on, an ugly and miserable old crone, in a cot on St. Hilary Down.

The Eastern bride of the lord of Pengersick was kind
and gentle to all with whom she had to do, and the lord
himself, it was said, was generous and helpful to all around ;
but he made no friendships nor held intercourse with those
of his own degree. The returned lord was, in fact, a lonely
and solitary man, riding forth alone and spending long hours
poring over strange books. His chamber, it is said, was full
of strange instruments, liquids and retorts, and as he laboured
with these in solitude the castle would be filled with strange
odours, which suggested the bottomless pit. At times as the
night wind howled round the turrets of the castle his voice
might be heard in the intervals of the blast summoning
spirits from the unseen world, and as they came in clouds
obedient to his bidding their voices were heard above the
beating of the waves on the rocks beneath and the howling
of the blast in the turrets. He was regarded by the people
as a white witch, whilst the witch of Fraddam was a black
witch and his antithesis. His spells were more powerful
than hers, and he at last drove her to sea in a coffin from
Germoe Churchyard, in which, as in a canoe, she could be seen
on stormy nights riding over the waves round Pengersick
Head, her wild, shrill shrieks of unholy laughter being
carried on the storm-wind.

The beautiful lady of Pengersick rarely ventured from
the castle ; and in summer time, it was said, she would sit
for hours with her casement open to the sea, like a true
Eastern lady, singing to the accompaniment of her harp the
softest, sweetest songs. At times fits of unutterable gloom
would settle down on the soul of her lord, and as David
with his harp lifted the darkness from the soul of Saul, so
this fair lady would soothe to rest the weary spirit of her
lord. Years drifted on, bringing but little change, till one
day there came a swarthy stranger of gloomy and forbidding
mien to Marazion, where he took up his abode. The fishermen would see him sometimes as the night closed in sitting

on the rocks overhanging the sea round Pengersick; or cottars would see him in the twilight wandering over the uplands. The lord of Pengersick went no more forth abroad, and a nameless dread seemed to have settled down on him and his lady. At last in the blackness of one awful night, in the midst of a terrible tempest that had risen up out of the Atlantic, a blaze of light shot up from the turrets of Pengersick Castle ; and in the morning a blackened heap of ruins alone marked the spot where it had stood, and the lord of Pengersick and his lady, and their Eastern servants and his beautiful steed, and the mysterious stranger of dark and awful mien were never heard of more.

Of course, it is difficult to collect the sediment of truth at the bottom of the foregoing legend. Perhaps we may conclude that some lord of Pengersick, whose old age was not accompanied by the proverbial wisdom of that state, as not infrequently happens, had fallen under the spell of a mercenary Delilah, and that in his infatuation he had allowed his son to be kidnapped by a gang of sea ruffians and carried abroad like Joseph of old, to be added to the hordes of Christian slaves that in those days dragged out a dismal existence at Tunis or Algiers. The spiriting away of the heir would thus leave the field open for the cherished plans and hopes of Delilah. History has a knack of repeating itself, and more slaves have risen to power and influence in the land of their bondage than the patriarch Joseph. Possibly the conscience of the heir of Pengersick was more elastic than that of many of his fellows, and he found it possible to recite the "*fateheh*" of Islam with reverence and *empressement*. In the fifteenth and sixteenth centuries there were many Christian renegades holding high positions in the service of the Mohammedan Powers of the Mediterranean—some of them Englishmen. Perhaps this may have been the career of the heir of Pengersick, ending in a return to his native land with riches, a bride of the daughters of Islam, and an Arab steed.

We may well ascribe the skin disease of his wicked step-mother to leprosy—then very common—rather than to the fumes of the witch's caldron. Adopting this rationalised interpretation of the legend, it is but natural to conclude that one who could thus readily exchange the creed for the "*fateheh*" had no deep inward convictions, and men without deep convictions are ever prone to embark upon the sea of speculation, and pursue such philosophic phantoms as the elixir of life and the philosopher's stone ; hence perhaps the strange instruments and the odours of the bottomless pit with which his name in tradition is associated.

Mr. Botterell, in his "Traditions and Hearth Stories of the West of Cornwall,"* gives a more copious account of this legend of Pengersick than the one here followed. He states that he heard the legend from the lips of an elderly man at Gwinear, who had often heard it related in the days of his youth. The main features of this story are, however, the same ; we have the additional statement in Mr. Botterell's legend that the old lord of Pengersick had himself in his youth been a soldier of fortune, and that the wander lust from time immemorial had been effervescent in the blood of the race. The legend runs that the old lord in the beginning of his days, as there were no wars at home, had betaken himself in search of loot and glory " to outlandish countries far away in the East, to a land inhabited by a people little better than savages, who instead of tilling the ground or digging for tin, passed the time in roving from place to place as they had need of fresh pasturage for their cattle, and that they lived in tents covered with the skins of their flocks, and that their raiment was made of the same material, and yet they had rich stores of jewels and gold, which they had obtained by the plunder of their more settled and industrious neighbours."

---

* Scenal Series, page 251.

It is said, most probably with truth, that St. Germoe's Chair was erected by some member of the Pengersick family, possibly as a peace-offering to Mother Church after some more than usually wild and lawless deed. The recess in the south chancel wall of Germoe Church, with its canopy of carved stone now meant to be used as sedilia, most probably was the tomb of some member of this restless race. This brief account of the Pengersick family may be closed with the prosaic statement that one of them represented Helston in Parliament in 1397 and again in 1406.

The manor of Pengersick in the reign of Henry VIII. passed by purchase to the family of Militon. The Militons descended from a daughter of the Pengersicks* it is interesting to note. According to Leland, Job Militou, the purchaser, came from Devonshire. On his arrival at Pengersick he set about building the present crumbling grey tower, which though sadly shorn of its former splendours dominates the valley. Hals, whose veracity is much open to doubt, states that Militou had fled to this remote corner of the world to hide his head and avoid avenging justice, having imbrued his hands in the blood of a fellow-man. Whether this deed was done by accident or with intent Hals does not say. It is more than probable that it was never done at all. The reason for the fortifying of the house of the Militons is not far to seek : it stands close to the sea, and the sea in those days was the open highway of all lawless spirits. Often from the summit of the grey Keep of Pengersick, in the years that followed its erection, might have been seen the sails of Barbary corsairs on the bosom of the sea. The crew of the merchantmen and the lonely fisherman in his little boat were alike eagerly snapped up by these marauders to swell the growing population of slaves in Tripoli and Algiers.

---

* See a paper by the Rev. T. Taylor on "The Bevilles of Drennick and Woolstan," No. LIV. Journal of the Royal Institution of Cornwall.

Under the shadow of night, when the sea was calm and the landing good, these rovers of the sea would steal inshore in open boats and surround some sleeping hamlet or farmhouse. The strong men were carried off to labour as slaves under the hot sun of Africa till death liberated them from their misery, whilst the portion that fell to the fair daughter was the listless ennui of the harem. The sea rovers were not the only danger that would menace the dwellers in Pengersick Castle in those days; the constant wars in which this country was embroiled would bring danger also from privateers, the licensed robbers of the sea. Spanish, French and Dutch men-of-war and privateers, each in turn would appear in the bay as the centuries drifted on. From generation to generation, down to the first fifteen years of this century, Mount's Bay echoed to the hoarse rumble of guns, and the cannon smoke of ships engaged in deadly conflict drifted over its waters; whilst numbers of lawless men, smugglers by repute and pirates* when occasion served, dwelt upon its shores. Well might the first Militou ensconce himself within the fortified walls of his Keep of Pengersick, considering the condition of the times in which he lived.

An extract from the State Papers for the year 1526 makes it clear that the ancient spirit of the wild Pengersicks was by no means absent from the souls of the Militons. A Portuguese ship had been wrecked at Gunwalloe and much cargo saved. The cargo was seized by the servants of Job Militon, second of the name at Pengersick, Thomas St. Aubyn and William Godolphin; when the unfortunate owner applied to the justices for redress he was told that such was the custom of the country, and that no redress of any kind was possible. It may be here mentioned that Job Militon was ultimately made Governor of St. Michael's Mount after the ill-starred rebellion of Humphrey Arundell.

---

* State Papers.

A fragmentary account of the ancient tower, before cruel neglect and decay had done their fatal work, may be of interest : " On the wainscot of the upper storey, which is curiously carved and painted, there are several quaint pieces of poetry, which are now nearly effaced. Beneath the painting of a blind man carrying a lame man on his back occur the lines :

> " The lame which lacketh for to go
>> Is borne upon the blinde's back,
> So naturally between them twoo,
>> The one supplied the other's lack.
> The blinde to laime doth lend his might,
> The laime to blinde doth yield his sight."

Under another painting, which represented the constant dripping of water upon a rock, the following lines are found :

> " What thing is harder than a rock !
> What softer than water clear !
> Yet will the same with often drop
>> The hard rock pierce, as doth appear.
> Even so nothing so hard to attayne,
> But may be had with labour and payne."

Other inscriptions and paintings in this ancient stronghold illustrated the blessedness of loyalty to the Sovereign and the happiness of the kingdom that is served by faithful and patriotic Ministers ; another the sacredness of the ties of marriage ; and yet another, under the representation of an ass laden with dainties and feeding upon thistles, the folly of the miser, who denies himself the necessaries of life and lays up store for others to wanton upon.

We can only deplore the spirit of neglect in generations that are gone that allowed this heritage of a former age to crumble and waste away by wind and rain and vandal hands. But for Dr. Borlase we should have never known of the former existence of the ancient frescos and their message of homely philosophy and truth.

A feature of Pengersick Tower is the numerous loop-holes for the discharge of arrows upon besiegers, and also the elaborate arrangement for pouring boiling pitch or lead upon assailants attacking the doors.

The race of Militou did not long continue owners of Pengersick. Job Militon, son of the purchaser, was succeeded by his son William Militon, who died without issue, leaving his inheritance to be divided amongst his six sisters ; the estate thus ultimately passed through the female line to the Godolphins and the Bullers.

Another ancient family owning considerable estates in the parish were the Sparnons, of Sparnon and Pengelly. They seem to have held their estates at any rate from the fifteenth century, if not earlier. We find from the Church registers that at the meridian of their prosperity they made alliances both with the Godolphins and the Arundells. The outlines of the ancient home of the Sparnons at Sparnon, under the shadow of the eastern end of Tregoning Hill, may still be traced, The Sparnons ultimately built themselves a larger house on higher ground at Pengelly, part of which still exists, serving as a farm house. In our Church and churchyard several of the memorials of the Sparnons still survive. Their estates were purchased in the eighteenth century by Mr, Justice Buller, and are still held by his descendant, the present Lord Churston. The Carter family settled in America, who in recent years have been such generous benefactors to Breage Church, descend on the female side from the Sparnons. It is pleasant to realise how frequently the offshoots of old families renew themselves in new lands, sending forth vigorous shoots to carry on old traditions and ideals of service and usefulness.

Worthies and Unworthies.

Harry Carter, John Carter, "King of Prussia"; "Smuggling Ways and Days; William Lemon, Captain Tobias Martin, Poet; Joseph Boaden, Mathematician.

CHAPTER VIII.

Harry Carter, smuggler, privateer and revivalist, was born on a small farm at Pengersick in 1749. His father, who was a miner by trade, eked out a livelihood, with the assistance of his sons and daughters, in farming a small plot of ground. Harry Carter tells us in his memoirs* that he was one of a family of eight sons and two daughters; that his eldest and youngest brothers received some scanty education at Germoe School, but that he and the rest of his family received no education beyond some crude home lessons in reading, given through the medium of the Bible. The problem of daily bread in the household of his parents was of much too pressing a nature to allow more than this in the way of education. As soon as strength permitted, the children had to go forth to work in the fields or the mines, that each might bring his share of daily bread to the common store. Though life was thus hard, the principles of religion were not neglected in the home, the children being taught to recite some prayers "after they were in bed" and to attend when possible the services at Germoe Church. His youth coincided with the strange stirrings in the religious life of the people brought about by the not infrequent peregrinations of John Wesley through the district. When Harry was eight years of age the soul of his brother Francis was touched

---

* "The Autobiography of a Smuggler," published by Messrs. Pollard, of Truro, 1894.

at one of those wild scenes of religious revivalism, and as the two brothers slept together, the little lad of eight became strangely impressed and awed by the change in the demeanour of his brother. He tells us, however, that these impressions of awe gradually faded out of his youthful mind. At ten he was sent to work at the mines on the surface, and he continued there for seven years, when he went to join his elder brothers in a more adventurous and stirring life upon which they had entered at Porthleah, soon to change its name to Prussia Cove.

Before we proceed further with the story of Harry Carter, it may be well to say something about Porthleah, so soon to become famous as a smugglers' haunt. Between Cudden Point on the west and Enys Point on the south lie three little coves. The one nearest to Cudden Point is called Pixies' Cove. This cove is too rocky and exposed to be used as a harbour, but its precipitous sides are riddled with caves suitable for the smugglers' trade. Next to Pixies' Cove comes Bessie's Cove, called after a wild character, Bessie Burrows, who there kept the Kiddlewink Inn, a famous rendezvous of the smugglers plying their lawless trade along the coast. Bessie's Cove is altogether hidden from view till the edge of the cliffs are reached which form its precipitous sides. A rugged road leads up the face of the cliff from Bessie's Cove, and at certain points in the ascent caves open into the recesses of the rocks. To the east of Bessie's Cove lies Porthleah, now known as Prussia Cove. The name Prussia Cove came to be given to it from John Carter, the elder brother of Harry, who soon came to be the acknow-ledged head of all the smuggling fraternity along the coast. In his youth John Carter had been the leader of his fellows in all boyish games, and stories of the great Frederick, King of Prussia, having penetrated to the remote West of Cornwall, had so fascinated the mind of this adventurous lad that he dubbed himself King of Prussia. This name not only stuck to him for the rest of his life, but it has stuck ever since to the little territory of Porthleah over which he ruled with an iron hand.

The occupation of the Carter brothers at Prussia Cove was nominally that of peaceful fishermen, but in reality that of daring smugglers. From this quiet and secluded nook in the coast Harry Carter began his career by making several voyages as supercargo of contraband in Folkestone and Irish luggers. Like so many men of his time and country anxious to make their way in the world, Harry Carter lost no opportunity of self-education, and rapidly made himself proficient in a rude system of accounts. At twenty-five he found himself in command of a small sloop of sixteen or eighteen tons and a crew of two men, busily engaged in the exciting trade of importer of contraband goods. The sun shone upon his illegal efforts, and so great was his success that he soon succeeded in making himself master of a sloop of thirty-two tons ; but his vaulting ambition aspired to still greater things, and the success that fortune so often extends to new and inexperienced players was still his. The sloop of thirty-two tons was quickly exchanged for one of fifty tons and a crew of ten men ; and this in its turn soon gave place to a heavily-armed cutter of sixteen guns and a crew of thirty-two men. At this time there seemed no cloud on his horizon, save gloomy religious thoughts that came welling up in his heart. He was greatly troubled about the sin of swearing and his lack of assurance that he was a " saved man," but not a whit about the dishonest and lawless nature of his calling. Having obtained from Government a licence to sail as a privateer in the American War, and with strict injunctions to his crew against all swearing on board, he set sail in December, 1777, in search of adventures and profit on a wider and more extensive scale ; but his star was no longer in the ascendant, and the favours of fickle fortune were to be denied him for many a long year. Off the French coast his bowsprit was carried away, and he put into St. Malo for repairs, little recking of the momentous transpirings since he had sailed from Penzance Bay ; for France had entered into alliance with the revolted American colonies, and was now at war with England. Carter thus sailed his heavily-armed cutter into a trap, out of which there was no escape. He and his men were made prisoners, and his ship and all that she contained became a French prize of war. "The King of Prussia," who happened to be on " business " at this time in the Channel Islands, hastened to his rescue, and attempted to explain matters to his captors. The attempt was a foolish one, and he soon found himself locked up with his brother Harry and the crew of the cutter in a French prison. Their captivity proved a hard and tedious one, but like the men of resource and purpose that they were, they at once set to work to make the best of their situation by learning the French language, whilst Harry, in addition, beguiled the ennui of his captivity by the study of navigation, which in after years served him in good stead. The two brothers did not obtain their liberty until after a captivity of two years, when freedom came to them in an exchange of prisoners.

Harry Carter on his return home refitted his old fifty-ton cutter and made several successful smuggling runs. One of these runs was attended with unpleasant consequences, which nearly proved disastrous. He had sailed to deliver a contraband cargo in South Wales ; on reaching the Welsh coast he left his cutter lying off the Mumbles whilst he landed to make final arrangements about running the cargo. In his absence the cutter was mistaken by a cruiser for one of the Dunkirk privateers, which at this time were haunting the Welsh coast like birds of prey, snapping up vessels engaged in the coasting trade. These privateers were for the most part commanded and manned, Carter tells us, by Irishmen. The crew of the cutter, seeing the cruiser bearing

down upon them, put out to sea to save their cargo of
contraband, and soon succeeded in eluding the cruiser by
superior speed. On giving up the chase the cruiser sent a
boat on shore, and Carter was arrested as the captain of the
Irish pirate. The matter ended in his being detained on
suspicion for twelve weeks, and his ultimate liberation was
only brought about by the representations of his Cornish
friends to the Admiralty. With the exception of this slight
overclouding of his horizon, things still continued for some
time to prosper with him. On his return home he informs
us that "he rode about the country getting freights and
collecting money for the 'company." Indeed, things
continued for some time to prosper so well with the
"company" that soon another large cutter of one hundred
and sixty tons, and carrying nineteen guns, was purchased by
them, whilst they gave orders for the building of a lugger
mounting twenty guns. These two vessels when fitted out
sailed, under the supreme command of Harry Carter, on
voyages of illicit merchandise. No wonder, under the
circumstances, Harry Carter began to fancy himself again,
as he tells us in his memoirs ; but there was, alas ! a fly in the
ointment. In the pride of his prosperity and self-satisfaction
swear words began continually to slip out of his lips ; this
weighed at times heavily on his soul and plunged him in
deep spiritual gloom. It was evidently words and not deeds
that counted in this man's creed.

His relations with the collector of Customs and preventive officers seem to have been of the most friendly character,
and herein lay most probably the secret of his success as a
smuggler ; indeed, the friendship of Carter with these officials
helps us to understand the cause of the extreme prosperity
of the smuggling industry along the Cornish coast at this
period. In December, 1780, Harry Carter was lying in
Newlyn Road aboard his cutter, with her consort the lugger
alongside, when a messenger came from his friend the

collector of Customs, saying that a Dunkirk privateer, called the Black Prince, and bearing a terrible reputation, was off St. Ives, committing many depredations upon the local shipping. The collector concluded his message by asking him to capture the privateer and so end the reign of terror along the coast. This duty was not at all to Harry Carter's liking; but, considering his business, it was a dangerous thing to displease the collector of Customs, and so with not a few qualms he set out upon the dangerous enterprise of actual warfare. He put round to St. Ives with his two vessels, and anchored off that town. On Christmas Day, in the morning, the redoubtable Black Prince hove in sight, and Carter sailed out of St. Ives Bay with his two ships to engage her. The Black Prince immediately put about and made for the open sea, a running fight ensuing between pursuers and pursued. The lugger in the pursuit soon received a fatal shot, which caused her to rapidly fill and sink with all hands on board. In the meantime Carter, having had his jib carried away by a shot and another planted in his hull, thought it high time to abandon the pursuit of the Black Prince ; he was thus able to bear up and rescue seventeen of the lugger's crew of thirty-one, but the rest found a watery grave. Carter tells us : " Before we came up with the privateer, in expecting to come to an engagement, oh ! what horror was on my mind for fear of death ! as I knew I must come to judgment sure and ' sartin.' I feared if I died I should be lost for ever. Notwithstanding all this I made the greatest outward show of bravery, and through pride and presumption exposed myself to the greatest danger. I stood on the companion until the wad of the enemy's shot flew in fire about me, and I suppose the wind of the shot struck me down on the deck, as the shot took in the mainsail right in a line with me. One of my officers helped me up and thought I was wounded, and he would suffer me to go there no more."

In 1786 Carter married Elizabeth Flindel, of Helford, and in the following year was born his only child, Elizabeth Carter. In January, 1788, happened the great disaster of his life. In attempting to land a cargo of smuggled goods in Cawsand Bay, he was surprised by boats sent off by a man-of-war. He and his crew attempted to offer an armed resistance ; the cutter was quickly boarded by the boat's crew, and Carter himself received a severe cutlass wound upon the head and was left lying upon the deck of his ship for dead. He was able to retain consciousness all the time, and when unobserved, with great difficulty, he managed to plunge into the water. Luckily he was seen by sympathisers on the shore, who only succeeded with great difficulty, on account of his wounded and exhausted condition, in bringing him safely to land. This adventure was to cost Carter dear, and it proved the culminating point in his career : henceforth the sun of good fortune only shone upon his path in fitful and watery gleams. In spite of the serious wound from which he was suffering, his friends managed in two days to bring him to the house of his brother Charles at Kenneggie, in Breage ; there he and his friends soon learnt the disquieting intelligence that the Government had offered a reward of £300 for his capture. It was now necessary for Carter, in order to avoid arrest, to be removed by night to Marazion. Soon the scent became too strong, and he again had to be removed in the dead of night to Acton Castle, then only occupied in the summer months by its owner, Mr. Stackhouse Pendarves. The land attached to this house was farmed by the " King of Prussia," who kept the keys of the house in the absence of the family. In this deserted mansion the wounded man had to lie in solitude for many weary months. It is said that the doctor who attended him in this retreat was brought blindfolded by night, and that on one occasion Carter only eluded justice by hastily assuming the garb of a woman. In this lonely refuge his disposition at once manifested its gloomy

morbidity and intense practicalness; much time seems to
have been profitably spent in the study of navigation, and
much wasted upon hypochondriacal maunderings upon the
condition of his soul, his occasional proclivity for swear
words and lack of assurance as to his state of salvation.
When his wounds healed he used to steal out of his lair at
night to Prussia Cove, returning ere the dawn. On one of
these occasions, as he returned he moralised on the singing
of the birds in the dawn "answering the end for which
they were sent into the world, so that I wished I had
been a toad or a serpent or anything, so that I had no
soul. Likewise there was a grey thrush which sang to
me night and morning, which have preached to me many
a sermon."

The sermons of this bird, like many other sermons, seem
to have produced no practical effect upon Carter's life. His
mind was utterly untroubled so far as the lawlessness of his
life was concerned, or the questionableness of many of his
deeds ; indeed, he made careful preparation for continuance in
lawless courses by the study of navigation.

In the autumn his wife was seized with rapid consump-
tion, and he paid a pathetic farewell visit to her under the
shadow of night at Helford, whither she had gone with her
little girl to be with her parents. He returned lonely
and broken-hearted to his refuge at Acton Castle a little
before the dawn, overwhelmed with the thought that he
would see his wife no more and that he was a ruined and
broken man.

On the 24th October, 1788, he was able to obtain a
passage to Leghorn on board the George, a ship sailing from
Penzance. From Leghorn he succeeded in obtaining a
passage to New York, where he became reduced to a condition
of extreme poverty, having for a bare pittance to work side
by side in the fields with negro slaves. After many hard-
ships he determined to brave the terrors of the law and

venture back once more to England. He worked his way back under the American flag, and narrowly escaped the attentions of the Press Gang in the English Channel. On his arrival in England he soon found that his native soil was still too hot for his feet. Under the circumstances he crossed over to Roscoff, on the French coast, the then capital of the Channel smuggling trade, where he became the local agent of his brothers. But events moved rapidly in France under the Revolution. During the Terror, with many other English, he was arrested and remained under detention for over two years. With the fall of Robespierre he and his other English fellow-prisoners were set at liberty. This smuggling Ulysses brought his wanderings to an end on the 22nd August, 1795. He disembarked on that day at Falmouth, he tells us, "at three o'clock in the afternoon, where I met my dear little Bessie, then between eight and nine years old." The following day happened to be Sunday, and he at an early hour set out for his native place, reaching Breage a little before eleven o'clock, and meeting his brother Frank on his way to church.

Harry Carter settled at Rinsey, became a farmer, and continued to reside there until the day of his death in April, 1829.

John Carter, known as "The King of Prussia," plays a much larger part in local tradition than his brother Harry, though on Harry fell the more onerous and dangerous part of facing the perils of the sea and of hostile shores in pursuit of the smuggler's calling. In those days and for long after the wild doings of Prussia Cove would be on everyone's lips; the doings on the lonely deep had no chronicler to magnify them. Many are the legends that cling round the name of "The King of Prussia": some of these Mr. Baring-Gould has placed on record in his book "Cornish Characters and Strange Events." On one occasion John Carter received a visit from the Revenue officers, who demanded to make a search of his entire premises. One door remained padlocked, and this they insisted on having opened; the key not being forthcoming they wrenched the locks off, but the cellar thus closed proved to be quite innocent of contraband. On the following day Carter complained to the Revenue authorities that his unlocked premises had been rifled during the night, and demanded restitution for his stolen goods, as the Revenue officers by their violent action had deprived him of the means of securing his doors. The story runs that Carter himself had removed his property during the night, and we are asked to believe the somewhat difficult statement that the Revenue officers under the circumstances paid him the value of the property he had never lost.

On another occasion we are told that the Revenue authorities seized in the cellars of Carter a valuable cargo of contraband spirits, which Carter had already made arrangements to supply to his customers amongst the surrounding gentry, and that on the following night Carter and his gang broke into the Custom warehouses, seized the contraband of which they had been deprived, and proceeded to deliver it to those for whom it had been originally intended.

His crowning exploit, however, was opening fire with a battery of guns which he had erected at Prussia Cove, on the boats of the Government cutter Faery. The Faery was in hot pursuit of a smuggling craft, which in order to elude her pursuer sailed through a narrow channel between the Enys rocks and the shore. The Faery, baffled of her prey, lowered her boats in pursuit, and as these drew into Prussia Cove, Carter opened fire upon them and beat them off. This seems to have been towards dusk. Next morning the Faery opened fire from the sea on Carter's shore battery, whilst mounted troops from Penzance took up their position on the shore to the rear of his battery, and in turn opened fire upon it. The smugglers thereupon withdrew to Bessie Burrow's public-house and prepared for its defence, but received no further attack or molestation. The whole incident as narrated reveals a strange supineness on the part of the Customs authorities, which almost suggests connivance with Carter's delinquencies.

The action of the authorities in the above case is reminiscent of a story told to the writer by a parishioner. His grandfather, who occupied a farmhouse on the coast, was awakened in the dead of night by a band of smugglers, who asked permission to stow a cargo of spirits, which they had just landed, in his barn under the straw. He demurred on the ground that if the cargo were discovered there by the authorities he would be incriminated, but he expressed willingness for it to be hidden in the hay ricks, contiguous to the barn. Some days afterwards his father, then a mere youth, was asked to assist in the disposal of some of the kegs, and, fearful of refusing, consented. Under cloak of night he set out with the smuggler, each bearing a keg; the way led over fields and by many devious paths till he found himself climbing the fence at the end of the garden of a Preventive officer living in Helston. He remonstrated with his guide at the madness of endeavouring to secrete contraband spirits in the garden of an Exciseman. In reply he was told to have no fear, but to do as he was told ; the fence was crossed and the keg was carried through the garden to the back door of the upholder of the law. The smuggler without trepidation proceeded to knock, and on the door being opened the kegs were placed inside without parley of any kind.

The grim side of the smuggler's calling and the terrible crimes that sometimes accompanied it are well illustrated by the gruesome find of another parishioner recently, close to his farmhouse, under the shadow of Tregoning Hill. The hind leg of one of the horses of this friend, whilst ploughing in his field, suddenly sank deep into the ground, and it was with difficulty that the animal was extricated. The spot from which the horse's foot was withdrawn revealed a cavity in the ground ; spades were brought and excavations made, which ended in bringing to light a fair-sized subterranean cellar, whose gruesome contents were a large knife of foreign make, a skull, a few human bones, some disintegrated patches of clothing and a small handful of silver and copper coins, one of which, a shilling of the reign of George II., now lies on the table of the writer.

From the Carters we turn to a man of a very different type, who made his way to wealth by sterling integrity and honesty of purpose. William Lemon was born at Germoe in 1696, and baptized in Breage Church on the 15th November of the same year. He received his education at the village school, and being a lad of quick intelligence, he became in the first instance a clerk to a Mr. Coster, connected with the local mining industry. He distinguished himself when a mere boy on the occasion of a ship being driven on Praa Sands in the midst of a terrific gale. He and a party of brave men, who arrived on the scene of the disaster as the ship was quickly breaking to pieces, formed themselves with great gallantry into a living chain, extending from the shore into the raging, angry surf, and so were able to grasp and save the shipwrecked sailors as they were carried on the waves to the shore. But for these heroic men thus grasping them they would have been sucked back into the sea and drowned in the receding waters. Young William Lemon was a lad of thoughtful and studious disposition, and availed himself of every opportunity to learn what there was to be learnt of assaying and mine engineering in the district. Presumably men of education and practical ability were very scarce in the neighbourhood at this time ; at any rate, whilst little more than a boy he was appointed the manager of considerable tin smelting works in the neighbourhood of Penzance. At the age of twenty-eight he married a Miss Isabella Vibart, of Tolver, in Gulval, a lady of some property. William Lemon was endowed with breadth of mind and grasp of detail in a marked degree, and the means which his wife brought him enabled him to bring these faculties into play with the most successful results. He embarked on prudent and far-sighted mining speculations, which quickly made him a man of great wealth. He conceived the idea of working the tin mines on a large scale, and not as hitherto by small bands or companies of "adventurers," as had been the custom for some generations.

Though great wealth came to him comparatively early, his character continued unchanged and unspoilt, and in the midst of his successes he continued to utilize his leisure in the study of Latin, and in his middle-age he had attained to no mean knowledge of that tongue. In the present age the successful developer of mines and floater of mining companies, spending his leisure in the study of the classics, would be indeed regarded as strange, but "*autres temps, autres mœurs.*"

When success came William Lemon settled in Truro. The kindliness of his character is well illustrated by an incident at this period of his life. He had trained a pet Cornish chough so well, and so fond had the bird become of him, that at his call it would leave its fellows and come and settle on his hand or his head as he walked along. A lad of the Truro Grammar School, named John Thomas, who afterwards became Warden of the Stannaries, accidentally killed this tame bird so dear to the heart of its owner. In fear and trembling he went to the house of Mr. Lemon, and confessed his crime. The lad's straightforwardness disarmed all resentment in the heart of this kindly man, who dismissed him with friendly words, after praising his openness and manliness of character in confessing his delinquency.

William Lemon served as High Sheriff of the county, and might have represented it in Parliament had he so chosen.[*] He ultimately bought the estate of Carclew, to which place he

---

[*]See Mr. Baring-Gould's "Cornish Characters and Strange Events" for many of the factors as given above.

went to reside in 1749. His son was created a baronet, and for some years represented Cornwall in Parliament. This baronetcy became extinct in the succeeding generation.

A friend has shewn the writer some letters of William Lemon, which reveal him as an affectionate and dutiful son to his aged mother, and kindly and solicitous for the welfare of all the members of his family. I venture to transcribe one of these letters, written to his brother at Germoe, who had been ailing for some time. It reveals a touching faith in the efficacy of alcohol as a restorer of the vigour of the human system, which the world has now lost, and also gives a quaint picture of a bygone age and generation.

The letter is as follows :—

" Truro,

28th September, 1748.

" Dear Brother,

I was much concerned to hear of the illness of you and your family, and consequently had great satisfaction in hearing of your being recovered. To comfort and recruit you, I have ordered to be brought you by this bearer four dozen bottles of wine, of different sorts, as mentioned on the other side, which I hope you will make use of with moderation. I cannot omit again pressing you to have particular attention to the education of your children. It will be surprising should you neglect this, seeing I have offered to contribute so much towards it. My good wishes attend you and your whole family, and I am

Your affectionate brother,

William Lemon."

" Bottles—4 Tent
,,   4 Canary
,,   12 Mountain
,,   28 Port
                ————
             48 Bottles."

It would not be right in a chapter dealing with the worthies and unworthies of Breage, who have stamped their memories beyond their fellows upon the local annals, to omit the name of "Captain" Tobias Martin. Although he was not actually a native of the parish of Breage, a great portion of his life was passed in the parish as captain of Wheal Vor Mine. He was born in the parish of Wendron on 5th January, 1747. His childish years, on account of the poverty of his father, a working miner, seem to have been practically destitute of all school education. Indeed, when we examine beneath the surface we find that a century ago in Western Cornwall school education of any kind seems to have stopped short with the children of the more well-to-do farmers. Young Tobias Martin, however, had inherited from his father an active and vigorous mind, which quickly set itself to grapple with the adverse circumstances of his surroundings. From a very early age he began to utilise all his spare time for the purpose of self-education, and in spite of long hours spent as a working miner, managed amongst other things to acquire a fair knowledge of Latin and written French. His father, in spite of the hard circumstances of his life, had possessed a genuine thirst for knowledge and information of all kinds, and tenderly preserved a few tattered and meagre volumes as a fountain of light and inspiration. He also possessed the faculty inherited by his son of stringing jingling rhymes together, which he regarded as endowed with the fire of genius. In his later years the father of Tobias Martin, on account of his integrity and superior education, was promoted by his employers to the post of mine captain.

The life of Tobias Martin practically followed the course of that of his father. After working for a number of years as an ordinary miner, his superior education and gifts came to be recognised by a Mr. Sandys, of Helston, interested in the local mines, and his advancement quickly followed. Tobias Martin died, aged 81, on 9th April, 1828, and was laid to rest in Breage Churchyard. The later years of his life were clouded by false accusations and unjust claims, which led for a time to his confinement in the Sheriff's Ward at Bodmin. His character was ultimately completely vindicated by the efforts of Mr. Richard Tyacke, of Godolphin. Hard upon this trouble followed the brutal murder of his eldest son in America, which darkened the few remaining years of the old man's life.

The poems of Tobias Martin were first published in Helston in 1831; a second edition followed in 1856, and a third in 1885. The poems suggest the mental attitude of an eighteenth century Cornish Piers Ploughman; running through them there is a vein of deep resentment at the tyranny and oppression of the ruling classes, and the lethargy, pride, hard-heartedness and laxity of the clergy is touched upon with no light hand. His verses as poetry are utterly valueless, but as garish pictures of a day that is passed they will always be interesting, if somewhat painful reading. Martin by his contemporaries was called an atheist. Judging by his poems, I imagine that he had thought perhaps a little more than his accusers, who most probably had never thought at all on the deeper things of life; his soul no doubt was in revolt against the dead shibboleths and formalism of the age, with which men were attempting to compound for the brutality and coarseness of their lives. One looks in vain through Martin's poems for one thought of poetic beauty or discernment.

Perhaps the following story of Martin, given by Mr. Baring Gould,[*] will suggest a picture of the man and his communications. It is fair to add that whilst the following story reveals him as a merry fellow, many of his poems reveal in him a strain of plaintive melancholy.

Captain Toby was having his pint of ale at a tavern,

---

[*] "Cornish Characters and Strange Events."

when in comes a miner who was wont to be called "Old Blowhard," and was not esteemed trusty or diligent as a workman.

"How are 'ee, Capp'n ? "

"Clever, how art thee ? "

"Purty well for health," says Bill, " but I want a job. Can 'ee give us waun ovver to yur new bal ? "

"No, we're full," replied Captain Toby.

"How many men have 'ee goat ovver theere ? " asked old Bill Blowhard.

"How many ? Why we've two sinking a air-shaft through the flockan, and two to taackle, and that's fower; and theere's two men in the oddit, and a booay to car tools and that, and that makes three moore, and that altogether es seben."

"And how many cappuns have 'ee goat ? " said Bill.

"How many ? Why ten."

"What ! Ten cappuns to watch ovver seben men ? I doant b'lieve you can maake. that out, for the venturers wouldn't stand it."

"Tes zackly so then, and I'll make it out to 'ee in a moment. Waun cappun es 'nough we oal knaw, but at the last mittin the 'venturers purposed to have waun of the 'venturers sons maade a cappun, and to larn, they said ; and so a draaper's son called Sems, was put weth me from school, at six pounds a month and a shaare of what we had in the 'count-house."

"Well, but how can 'ee maake ten of you and he ? "

"Why I'll tell 'ee how, and you mind nother time Bill, for theere's somethin' of scholarin' in ut. Now see this. I myself am waun, baent I ? "

"Iss sure," said Bill.

"Well, and theest aught to knaw that young Sems is nawthin'; well when theest ben to school so long as I have, theest knaw that waun with a nought attached to un do maake ten, and so 'tes zackly like that."

I venture to give one specimen of Tobias Martin's poetry.

" Awake, my soul ! the night is past,
　　The day begins to dawn,
　With eager footsteps let me haste
　　To meet the rising sun.

" But first to heaven's exalted throne
　　A tribute let me pay,
　To Him who hath His mercies shewn,
　　And sent another day.

" To honest labour then inclined
　　I'll hasten to the spot,
　With cheerful and contented mind,
　　Where heaven hath cast my lot.

" And there let me my daily task
　　With busy hands pursue,
　And God's assistance humbly ask
　　In all I have to do.

" Though some despise my mean estate,
　　I would not have it said
　I spend my time in sloth and hate,
　　Nor earn my daily bread.

" While idle wretches pine and starve,
　　And nothing good will do,
　I'll labour on and try to serve
　　God and my neighbour to."

It would be unjust not to make mention in concluding this chapter of Joseph Boaden, who lived his whole life as a small cultivator in the parish of Breage, and who was laid to rest in Breage Churchyard in December, 1858. Self-taught, through his life he pursued the study of higher mathematics and astronomy, and was regarded as a valued correspondent by Professors Airy and Adams, of Cambridge. Under modern conditions education has become more diffused, but we look in vain for men of the type of those whom we have been considering. With its superficial diffusion knowledge has in a measure lost its prestige and fascination, and education has been in a sense debased and vulgarised in the popular mind into a mere instrument of livelihood. The successful passer of competitive examinations, under the system of cram, with no true love of knowledge for knowledge's sake in his heart, and who divests himself of his crapula of potted knowledge the moment a livelihood with a pension at the end has been attained, has already gone far to cast learning, so far as the popular mind is concerned, into the quagmire of contempt.

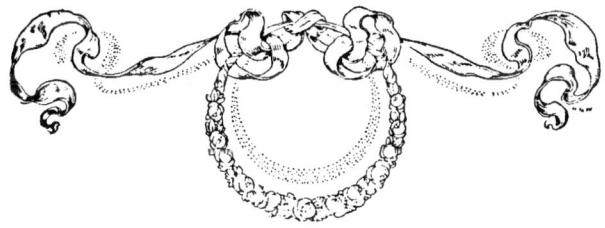

Local Place Names and Superstitions.

CHAPTER IX.

It has been said that the history of England is written in the names of her fields and enclosures. Certain it is that in almost. every parish, if the names of the fields be gone over, some name of exceeding interest or curiousness will be discovered, embalming some long-forgotten fact or tradition. There are in the parish of Breage two fields called " The Sentry " ; this name is of course obviously a corruption of the word "sanctuary." These two sanctuary fields are at opposite ends of the parish ; one forms the site of the main shaft of Wheal Vor Mine, and the other is in the Kenneggie district. Their situation thus lends force to a suggestion that they may in remote times have been actually used as local sanctuaries.* The probability of this seems to be increased by the fact that a field contiguous to the Kenneggie sanctuary field, is called the Church Close. Possibly in ancient days in the Church Close there stood a sanctuary chapel, whose story has long since faded into the mists of oblivion. Originally every church and churchyard was a sanctuary for criminals. The sanctuary seats at Hexham Abbey and Beverley Minster and the sanctuary knocker in Durham Cathedral are still in existence. A person who had committed murder or other heinous crime was safe if he could reach a sanctuary before he was waylaid and arrested ; once within the sanctuary, if in forty days he confessed his crime and took a solemn oath before the coroner to depart from the country and never

---

* I am aware that the term Sanctuary came to be applied very loosely, and came to mean sometimes little more than Churchland or even a Tithe Barn. The Rev. Thomas Taylor, of St. Just, suggests with regard to the Kenneggie "Church Close" and "Sanctuary" that these fields may have been fragments of the ancient Manor of Methleigh, which passed from the See of Exeter to the Dean and Chapter of Exeter, who alienated it from the Church.

return again, he was allowed to go unmolested into exile. Possibly our two local sanctuaries may have been thus used in Celtic times. Had they continued to be used as such in later times, it is probable that some record of this use would have survived.

Two fields in the parish possess the gruesome name of " Park Blood." Certain local antiquaries have drawn the conclusion that the numerous fields of Blood dotted over West Cornwall commemorate the sites of desperate tribal struggles. It seems much more probable and reasonable, however, that " Park Blood " * is merely the corruption of the ancient Cornish for " Field of Flowers." This derivation, it is fair to add, seems in keeping with a number of other local names of fields, as " Eye Bright Field," " Bramble Field," " Furzy Croft Field," tc.

Another field of somewhat gruesome name is " Venton Ghost." Mr. Jenner suggests that this name may be a corruption of " Well of Blood," a title which may well have been due to the red waters of a chalybeate spring.

From a field whose name naturally suggests at a first sight ghosts and hauntings, we pass naturally to a field which bears the portentous name of " Wizard's Plot " ; alas ! all memory of the wizard who once probably dwelt on this spot, and practised his spells and necromancy there, has long since faded into oblivion.

It would be interesting to know how a field on Methleigh Farm obtained the name of " The Martyr's Close." As to who these martyrs were tradition can give no light. It is possible that the name may commemorate one of the many acts of ferocity committed in the name of religion in the days of the " Saints," when slight religious differences were ample

---

* " Park Blood " might be " Park Blod." the field of flowers   " Blodon ". in the 12th century vocabulary is " Flos," and " Blot " is the same as ' ' farina." In Welsh " blawd " is " flour " and " blodon " " flower." In later Cornish " blez " is " flour " and " bledzahn " is " flower." There still survives a dialect word " blouth."

Mr. H. Jenner

justification for any form of homicide, or it may have had, as seems more probable to the writer, some connection with the story of the unfortunate men whose skeletons, bearing upon them the unmistakable traces of violent death, were discovered lying in a shallow grave beneath the site of the pulpit in Breage Church. If this latter theory be accepted it seems probable that the field earned its present name through some act of military reprisal during the Parliamentary Wars.

In the Germoe district there is a field called " Bargest Croft." At first sight " Bargest " suggests a corruption of " Bargheist," * the Teutonic and Scandinavian animal spectre, whose apparitions play such a large part in the folklore of the North of England. The resemblance in the words, however, is only superficial, " Bargest " evidently being a corruption of " Bargas," a kite, which is a more or less common form in compound local place names.

Turning from place names which have been culled in the main from the tithe map to the parish tithe itself. Probably our tithe with other Cornish tithe came first to be paid in Celtic times, not through any force of law, but gradually by custom, each owner of land making what was deemed a fitting payment for the maintenance of the bishop and clergy of the diocese and possibly to some extent for the relief of the poor. As in so many other instances long custom came gradually to obtain the force of legal enactment and the payment of tithe to become legally binding. When Churches were built at Breage and Germoe, our local tithe instead of going to the support of the clergy of the diocese generally, would pass to the special use of the clergy of Breage and Germoe ; the right of appointing such clergy passing also by custom, it seems more than probable, to the builders of the Churches and their heirs.

When we deal with the fast fading superstitions of the

---

* Mr. H. Jenner.

district, it is interesting to note the extreme frequency in local folklore of superstitions exactly parallel to the Northern superstition of the Bargheist. At no very distant time, judging from the accounts of the aged, the majority of the lanes, roads and lonely places of the district were inhabited by spectral animals. The Board School master, however, has been allowing them no close time, and they soon will be as extinct as the mammoth, the cave bear, or the woolly haired rhinoceros. It is considered unlucky locally to behold these spectral animals, just as in the Northern superstitions the appearance of the Bargheist denotes disaster to the beholder. A flock of phantom sheep on the main road have not yet been quite exterminated, and their pitter-patter on wild, stormy nights may still be heard by the belated wayfarer, whilst a little further on, closely contiguous to the main road, it is said a phantom "passun" may still be seen ; also certain houses have been pointed out to the writer as having been terribly troubled with "sperruts."

The great enemy of "sperruts" and spectres of all kinds in his day was the Reverend Robert Jago,[*] Vicar of Wendron, at the end of the seventeenth century. The dim traditions of his doughty feats in warring with spectres still vaguely linger, in a condition varying. towards evanescence, in the popular mind. A lane leading up from the village of Herland Cross to Pengilly Farm still bears the name of Jew's Lane. In this lane a Jew had hanged himself in rage or despair after some outrage or wrong committed upon him by the Squire Sparnon of that day. Not long after the Jew's suicide the lane was rendered impassable at night by horrible sounds and sights, and recourse was had to the Reverend Robert Jago, who received a fee of five guineas for the business of laying the troublesome ghost. The method of Mr. Jago seems to have been first to draw a circle with a long whip-

[*] See Daniell's "History of Cornwall."

lash upon the ground, whilst repeating certain formulæ and prayers. Having placed himself within the circle, he was safe from the anger of malignant spirits, and was thus able to summon the troubled spirit and banish it from the neigbour-hood without danger to himself.

Mr. Wentz, in his " Faery Faith of Celtic Countries," gives the following story, taken from the lips of an aged man—John Wilmet, of Constantine—having reference to Parson Jago and the traditions of ghost-laying that still linger round his name : " A farmer who once lived near the Gweek River called Parson Jago to his house to have him quiet the ghosts and spirits regularly haunting it, for Parson Jago could always put such things to rest. The parson went to the farmer's house, and with his whip formed a circle on the floor, and demanded the spirit, which made its appearance on the table, to come down into the circle. Whilst on the table the spirit was visible to all the family, but as soon as it got into the ring it disappeared and the house was never troubled afterwards."

John Wilmet had also much to tell Mr. Wentz about the piskies or pobol vean. that he heard, but did not see, at Bosahn. It is round the piskies, indeed, that the great mass of Cornish folk beliefs cling. Sixty or seventy years ago this belief seems to have been all but universal amongst the country people, and though now fast dying, is by no means extinct. Indeed, a churchwarden of many years standing recently dated a certain event by the winter in which he had been piskie " led." It seems on this occasion when leaving the market town he had taken the wrong turning and walked on rapidly till in the end he found himself more than twelve miles from home. Another Cornishman informed the writer that one night, thinking something was disturbing some of his cattle, he went out into his field to see what was the matter ; when he endeavoured to return to the house, owing to the piskies he could not find the gate again, and had to spend several weary hours wandering round and round the hedges in a vain and exasperating search in rain and darkness, at one time floundering in a nettle bed, at another in mud and water over the tops of his boots.

An aged woman, Mrs. Harriet Christoper, informed Mr. Wentz, that a woman who lived near Breage Church had a fine baby, and she thought the piskies came and took it and put a withered child in its place. The withered child lived to be twenty years old, and was no larger when it died than when the piskies brought it. The parents believed that the piskies often used to come and look over the wall by the house to see the child, and she had heard her grandmother say that the family once put the child out of doors at night to see if the piskies would take it back again. The piskies are said to be very small, and you could never see them by day. She used to hear her grandmother, who had been dead fifty years, say that the piskies used to hold a fair in the fields near Breage, and that the people saw them dancing. She also remembered her grandmother saying that it was customary to set out food for the piskies at night.

Mr. Hunt, in his popular "Romances of the West of England," tells us that Bal Lane in Germoe was a famous haunt of the fairies in old time, and that at certain seasons of the year they held a great fair there.

The fairy folk in local superstitions seem to have been divided into three species—the piskies, fairies of the moors, dells and surface of the earth generally ; the knockers or knackers, fairies of the mines, whom the miners heard knocking in the depths of the earth, indicating by their knocks the presence of rich veins of ore, or if of a malignant disposition luring the miners by their knockings to vain efforts after non-existent mineral wealth. The third order of fairies was that of the Buccas, an amphibious species, to whom down to recent times offerings of fish were made.

It is pleasant to gather from the learned author of "The

Faery Faith in Celtic Countries" that the superstitions of the Cornish are of a much brighter character than those of the other branches of the Celtic race; the superstitious beliefs of their near kinsmen, the Bretons, being of a specially gloomy character. The pobol vean, it seems, are much more cheery folk, in spite of all their pranks, than gloomy Ankou, king of the dead, and his attendant ghosts. Having said that the Cornish folklore is not of a gloomy character is to say perhaps all that can be said in praise of it.

I have alluded to the foregoing tales and beliefs because in the course of a generation or so they will have completely faded from the popular mind. Our people seem eager to have done with the past, and to reach forward to the future, fraught with new conditions and new thought. When we compare the present with the past, we can only be thankful for all that change has brought within recent generations in physical surroundings and moral outlook. Let us hope that her future gifts, which give promise of being prodigal, will be as beneficent as those of the recent past, for we still require much at her hands. The danger seems to lie in wandering into a materialistic desert, for it is but too true that "Man can not live by bread alone."

INDEX.

A.

B.

O

P.

R.

S.

T.